ASPECTS OF EARLY ENGLISH DRAMA

ASPECTS OF
EARLY ENGLISH DRAMA

Edited by Paula Neuss

D. S. BREWER · BARNES & NOBLE

© *Contributors 1983*

First published 1983 by
D. S. Brewer, 240 Hills Road, Cambridge,
an imprint of Boydell & Brewer Ltd
PO Box 9, Woodbridge, Suffolk IP12 3DF.
and by Barnes & Noble
81 Adams Drive, Totowa, NJ 07512

ISBN 0 85991 137 3

British Library Cataloguing in Publication Data

Aspects of early English drama.
1. Mysteries and miracle plays, English—History
and criticism
I. Neuss, Paula   822'.0516   PR1260

ISBN 0-85991-137-3

Library of Congress Cataloguing in Publication Data

Main entry under title:
Aspects of early English drama.
Includes bibliographical references and index.
1. English drama—To 1500—History and criticism—
Addresses, essays, lectures.   2. Mysteries and miracle-
plays, English—History and criticism—Addresses, essays,
lectures.   3. Theater—England—History—Medieval,
500–1500—Addresses, essays, lectures.   I. Neuss, Paula.
PR641.A86   1984   822'.0516'09   83-21331
ISBN 0-389-20428-5

Printed by Nene Litho, Wellingborough, Northants.
Bound by Woolnough Bookbinding, Wellingborough, Northants.

Contents

List of Illustrations

Plates 1, 2, 3 and 5 and figures 1, 2 and 3 by permission of the British Library; plate 4 by permission of the Master and Fellows of St. John's College, Cambridge; plate 6 by permission of Tessa Musgrave; plate 9 by permission of the Bodleian Library.

Preface

E. M. Forster chose 'Aspects' as part of a title 'because it is unscientific and vague'. While none of the work here is either of these, there is something to be said for a title that 'leaves us the maximum of freedom'. Again and again this book's authors have remarked on how difficult it is to pontificate about what we used to call 'medieval' drama.

I used to begin my lectures on 'medieval drama' with a list of things people would probably have heard that were not really true, but students understandably found this confusing. So I shall simply say here that almost every assumption that used to be made about Early English ('Pre-Shakespearian') Drama (including the classification of it as 'medieval') has had to be questioned in the light of recent research. The two most important new areas of work are the systematic scrutiny of all surviving records relating to the original productions and imaginative experimental *modern* productions based on careful treatment of the surviving texts. Both the *REED* project, which 'aims to find, transcribe, and publish external evidence of dramatic, ceremonial and minstrel activity in Great Britain before 1642' and the *PLS (Poculi Ludique Societas)* which sponsors productions of early plays through an approach combining 'research and experiment', are based in Toronto, where twenty years ago I attended a postgraduate seminar run by John Leyerle and played Lady Science in the first *PLS* production. The English equivalents are the Malone Society, which has reprinted several sets of dramatic records, most recently those of Norfolk and Suffolk; the Leeds School of English, which is producing facsimiles of the play manuscripts in its Texts and Monographs series, and the Medieval Players, a professional touring company based in the Goswell Road in Clerkenwell, near where pageants were performed in Chaucer's time.

These two areas of research form the basis of this book. Most of the authors have worked closely both with original records and texts and modern productions, and both are illustrated in the plates. The plays are approached from a practical angle, with a consideration of the details of music, stage management, costume and stage machinery. The first five chapters are mainly concerned with mystery plays, chapter six with saints plays, and chapter seven with morality plays, but we have all been conscious of the limitations of these generic subdivisions, and chapters eight and nine deal with characters and themes of late medieval drama in general. And although we have concentrated on 'Early English' drama, comparisons are made with continental drama, late medieval poetry and later playwrights, especially Shakespeare.

Whatever 'medieval' once implied, we now know that these plays were carefully contrived works of art. ('Folk' drama may be another matter: for information on this the reader is referred to Alex Helm's book *The English Mummers Play*, Boydell and Brewer, 1980.) The 'craft' that Noah's Ark symbolizes was believed to have been divinely inspired: the 'werk' was done to God's glory but it was also 'pley'. This book is structured on similar lines to some of the original plays: it begins with music and ends with a debate about Justice and Mercy, and there are many diversions on the way. Like the original playwrights, the writers aim to entertain as well as instruct, to provide both 'sentence and solaas' as Chaucer put it.

I must record my particular thanks to Meg Twycross and Peter Meredith for creating *Medieval English Theatre*, a series of annual meetings accompanied by a lively journal that publishes new research in the field. It was at their 1980 conference in Leeds that I first met several of the authors of this book. I should like to thank all the contributors for their promptness and patience, qualities (like scholarship and a sense of theatre) not frequently combined. I am also grateful to Diana Godden for her assistance in preparing this book and to Graham Handley for work on the Index.

Paula Neuss
Birkbeck College
1982

ABBREVIATIONS

Bakere	Jane Bakere, *The Cornish Ordinalia: A Critical Study* (Cardiff, University of Wales Press, 1980).
Barclay	Alexander Barclay, *The Ship of Fools*, ed. T. H. Jamieson, Vol. 1 (Edinburgh, 1874).
Beadle and Meredith	Richard Beadle and Peter Meredith, 'Further External Evidence for Dating the York Register (BL Additional MS 35290)', *Leeds Studies in English*, NS XI (1980), pp. 51–8.
Brewer and Gairdner	J. Brewer, J. Gairdner and R. Brodie, *Letters and Papers, Foreign and Domestic, of the Reign of Henry VIII*, 21 vols. (London, 1862–1910).
Chambers	E. K. Chambers, *The Mediaeval Stage*, 2 vols. (Oxford, 1903).
'Chelmsford'	John C. Coldewey, 'The Digby Plays and the Chelmsford Records', *Research Opportunities in Renaissance Drama*, XVIII (1975), pp. 103–121.
Chester	*The Chester Mystery Cycle*, ed. R. M. Lumiansky and David Mills, Vol. 1 (London (EETS), 1974).
Chester, Bodley Facsimile	*The Chester Mystery Cycle: A Facsimile of MS Bodley 175*, with an introduction by R. M. Lumiansky and David Mills, Leeds Texts and Monographs, Medieval Drama Facsimiles I (The University of Leeds School of English, 1973).
Chester, Harley Facsimile	*The Chester Mystery Cycle: A Facsimile of MS Harley 2124*, with an introduction by R. M. Lumiansky and David Mills, Leeds Texts and

Monographs, Medieval Drama Facsimiles VIII (Leeds School of English, forthcoming).

Chester, Huntington Facsimile | *The Chester Mystery Cycle: A Reduced Facsimile of Huntington Library MS 2*, with an introduction by R. M. Lumiansky and David Mills, Leeds Text and Monographs, Medieval Drama Facsimiles VI (The University of Leeds School of English, 1980).

Cohen | Gustave Cohen, *Histoire de la Mise en scène dans le Théâtre réligieux français du moyen age*, 8 vols. (Paris, 1906).

Coventry | *Two Coventry Corpus Christi Plays*, ed. Hardin Craig (London (EETS), 1957).

Drama and Art | Clifford Davidson, *Drama and Art*, Early Drama, Art and Music Monograph Series I (Kalamazoo, 1977).

Digby | *The Late Medieval Religious Plays of Bodleian MSS Digby 133 and E Museo 160*, ed. D. C. Baker, J. L. Murphy and L. B. Hall, Jr. (Oxford (EETS), 1982).

Feuillerat *Elizabeth* | *Documents relating to the Office of the Revels, in the Time of Queen Elizabeth* ed. A. Feuillerat (Materialien zur Kunde des alteren Englischen Dramas XXI, ed. W. Bang, Leuven 1908, reprinted Kraus, Liechtenstein, 1968).

Giradot | A de Giradot, *Mystère des Actes des Apôtres Répresenté à Bourges en Avril 1536* (Paris, 1854).

JEGP | *Journal of English and Germanic Philology*.

Kahrl | Stanley Kahrl, *Traditions of Medieval English Drama* (London, 1974).

Linthicum | M. Channing Linthicum, *Costume in the Drama of Shakespeare and his Contemporaries* (Oxford, Clarendon Press, 1936).

Macro | *The Macro Plays*, ed. Mark Eccles (London (EETS), 1969).

Malone VII	*Malone Society Collections Volume VII: Records of Plays and Players in Kent 1450–1642* ed. Giles E. Dawson (OUP, 1965).
Malone VIII	*Malone Society Collections VIII: Records of Plays and Players in Lincolnshire 1300–1585* ed. Stanley J. Kahrl (OUP 1974 for 1969).
Malone IX	*Malone Society Collections IX:* containing 'A Corpus Christi Play and other Dramatic Activities in Sixteenth Century Sherborne, Dorset' by A. D. Mills (OUP, 1977 for 1971).
Malone XI	*Malone Society Collections XI: Records of Plays and Players in Norfolk and Suffolk 1330–1642* ed. David Galloway and John Wasson (OUP 1980/1).
MED	*Middle English Dictionary.*
ME Sea Terms	Sandahl, Bertil, *Middle English Sea Terms*, 2 vols. (Uppsala, 1951, 1958).
METh	*Medieval English Theatre.*
'N-Town'	*Ludus Coventriae or The Plaie called Corpus Christi*, ed. K. S. Block (London (EETS), 1922).
'N-Town' Facsimile	*The N-Town Plays: A Facsimile of British Library MS Cotton Vespasian DVIII*, with an introduction by Peter Meredith and Stanley J. Kahrl, Leeds Texts and Monographs, Medieval Drama Facsimiles IV (The University of Leeds School of English, 1977).
Non-cycle Plays	*Non-cycle Plays and Fragments*, ed. Norman Davis (London (EETS), 1970).
Norris	*The Ancient Cornish Drama*, ed. Edwin Norris, 2 vols. (Oxford, 1859).
NQ	*Notes and Queries.*
OED	*Oxford English Dictionary.*
Piers Plowman	*Langland's Vision of Piers the Plowman*, ed. W. W. Skeat (London (EETS), 1869; pt. II, B-text, used unless otherwise stated).

PMLA	*Publications of the Modern Language Association of America.*
REED	*Records of Early English Drama.*
REED Coventry	*Records of Early English Drama: Coventry*, ed. R. W. Ingram (University of Toronto Press, 1981).
REED Chester	*Records of Early English Drama: Chester*, ed. Lawrence M. Clopper (Manchester University Press, 1979).
REED York	*Records of Early English Drama: York*, ed. Alexandra F. Johnston and Margaret Rogerson, 2 vols. (Manchester University Press, 1979).
RES	*Review of English Studies.*
Robbins	*Historical Poems of the XIVth and XVth Centuries*, ed. R. H. Robbins (New York, 1959).
RORD	*Research Opportunities in Renaissance Drama.*
Salter	F. M. Salter, *Medieval Drama in Chester* (Toronto, 1955).
Sharp	Thomas Sharp, *A Dissertation on the Pageants or Dramatic Mysteries Anciently Performed at Coventry* (Coventry, Merridew, 1825).
Towneley	*The Towneley Plays*, ed. G. England and A. Pollard (London (EETS), 1897).
Towneley Facsimile	*The Towneley Cycle: A Facsimile of Huntingdon MS HM I*, with an introduction by A. C. Cawley and Martin Stevens, Leeds Texts and Monographs, Medieval Drama Facsimiles II (The University of Leeds School of English, 1976).
Tydeman	W. Tydeman, *The Theatre in the Middle Ages* (Cambridge, 1978).
Wickham	Glynne Wickham, *Early English Stages*, Vol. 1 (London, 1963).
Woolf	Rosemary Woolf, *The English Mystery Plays* (London, 1972).

Wright   *Political Poems and Songs relating to English History*, ed. T. Wright, 2 vols. (London, 1859).

York   *The York Plays*, ed. Richard Beadle (London, 1983).

York Facsimile *The York Play: A Facsimile of MS Additional 35290*, with an introduction by Richard Beadle and Peter Meredith, Leeds Texts and Monographs, Medieval Drama Facsimiles VII (Leeds School of English, 1983).

'Alle Hefne Makyth Melody'

Richard Rastall

A reading of any substantial body of early English religious drama shows that music played an important part in it. Looking through the Chester or N-Town plays, for instance, we find many stage directions demanding music: and a close reading of the text itself reveals other places where music is required. In looking for a rationale to explain the use of music in the plays, we must reject the nineteenth-century concept of 'incidental music' directed at the emotions. Instead, we should identify the philosophical traditions – those ways of thought that were common in the Middle Ages – that seem to inform the plays and their use of music.

We may begin by considering the functions of music in the plays as shown by the stage directions and textual references. The first set of functions is that in which music acts as part of the *representation* of characters and locations associated with them. As John Stevens noted, music in the biblical plays most often represents Divine Order, the music being attached to God himself and to the workings of his universe.[1] The angels sing as soon as they are created ('N-Town', p. 17; *Chester*, p. 4): and there is minstrelsy at the expulsion of Adam and Eve from Paradise after the Fall (*Chester*, pp. 29, 31) because Divine Order is restored in the Garden. Although instrumental music is never named, the vocal music is often referred to by its title in the stage directions, and in almost every case can be identified as a liturgical piece. Occasionally a stage direction seems to specify a complete text to be sung:

> *hic cantent angeli in celo.* ¶ *Tibi omnes angeli tibi celi et universe potestates · Tibi cherubyn et seraphyn incessabili voce proclamant · Sanctus · Sanctus · Sanctus · Dominus deus sabaoth.*
>
> ('N-Town', p. 17)
> (Here the angels will sing in Heaven: 'To thee all Angels cry aloud: the Heavens, and all the Powers therein. To thee Cherubin, and Seraphin: continually do cry, Holy, Holy, Holy: Lord God of Sabaoth.')

This tells us precisely how much of the *Te Deum* is to be sung, whereas the

1

stage directions in the parallel York play (where only incipits are given) are less informative (*York*, pp. 49, 50).

The musical representation of Heaven occurs also at moments of divine intervention in human affairs. In the York play of the Annunciation, for instance, the angel's message to Mary is twice prefaced by his singing (*York*, p. 114: cf Peter Meredith, p. 23 below). Here the music helps to show the heavenly nature of the messenger, and thus to clarify the dramatic situation.

It is not obvious to a twentieth-century audience that music should characterize Divine Order: that it does so is a reflection of the standard cosmology of the Middle Ages as transmitted by Boethius (c. 480 – c. 524) from the works of Pythagoras and Plato. The common belief was that the universe was founded on the simple mathematical proportions that also gave rise to the musical consonances. Indeed, the universe in its motions was thought to produce harmonious sounds, the Music of the Spheres (*musica mundana*), although these sounds could not be heard by the ears of sinful man. Thus music was not only a strong metaphor for Divine Order but – in the singing and playing of angels – a representation of it. This tradition did not belong exclusively to drama, but can be seen also in paintings and carvings. If we look at a picture of the Assumption and Coronation of the Virgin, or examine the angelic minstrels in the roof of Manchester Cathedral or the choir arches at Lincoln (and there are many other examples), we are drawn to the conclusion that medieval man expected Heaven to be peopled with musical angels, both singing and playing instruments. Thus the depiction of Heaven as a musical place in the plays – specifically, as a place where the Creator is praised and joy can be expressed through music – is part of a widely-held belief that helps to explain the power of the dramatic use of music. When the Archangel Michael concludes the N-Town play of the Assumption with

> Now blysid be youre namys we cry
> ffor this holy assumpcyon · alle hefne makyth melody

('N-Town', p. 373, and the source of my title for this chapter), the playwright is making use of a tradition more powerful and more deeply ingrained in the medieval consciousness than we might at first think.

In all this heavenly music, however, God the Father never sings, for the Creator does not praise himself. Even Christ sings only rarely: and on the one certain occasion when he does so it is as the incarnate Son, not as the Creator:

> Ascendo ad Patrem meum et Patrem vestrum,
> Deum meum et Deum vestrum. Alleluya.
> (*Chester*, p. 373)
> ('I go up to my Father and your Father, to my God and your God. Alleluya'.).

2

A second type of music in the Boethian cosmology was *musica humana*, also the result of harmonious proportions in the universe, but on a smaller scale. It included the relation between man's body and his soul. Thus it is the godly characters, whose body and soul are most harmoniously related and who are therefore most in tune with the Divine Will, who are most musical in the plays. (Even now we use musical metaphors for these matters.)

The singing of mortals in the plays, then, is a positive means of identifying those who are instruments of the Divine Will. That is why such characters as the family of Noah, the Virgin Mary, Simeon and the Apostles all sing. The shepherds at the Nativity are musical, too, and keen enough to discuss the merits of the angelic *Gloria*. In the Chester Shepherds' play the boy Trowle rebukes his three masters, giving their 'sittinge withowt any songes' as part of his reason for not joining them (*Chester*, p. 134). This is not wholly deserved, for when they have discussed the angelic *Gloria* the shepherds are moved to sing a 'mery songe us to solace', as the Second Shepherd says (*Chester*, p. 145). Nevertheless, it is Trowle who turns their abilities to a more godly use, suggesting a joyous song in praise of the Christ-child and thus initiating an overt imitation of the mirthful angelic music in Heaven:

> And singe we all, I read,
> some myrth to his majestee,
> for certayne now see wee it indeede:
> the kinge Sone of heavon is hee.
> (*Chester*, p. 146)

Musica humana and the imitation of angelic music give us two good reasons why God's chosen mortals tend to be musical in the plays. The same reasons hold for those souls who will ultimately take their place in Heaven. The patriarchs and prophets in Limbo sing of their hope in God before the Harrowing of Hell, and again in praise of him after it; and the Saved Souls sing after the Judgement.

The great majority of musical items in the mystery plays are best understood in the ways just described: but there is another use of music – most common in the moralities and interludes, but found in the mystery plays also – that seems to demand a different interpretation. The singing of the 'Good' Gossips in Chester Play III clearly is not the musicality of godly persons; nor, presumably, is Herod entitled to minstrelsy for the same reasons that God is (*Chester*, p. 52; *Coventry*, p. 19; 'N-Town', pp. 152 and 176). Stevens explained such music in terms of realism, but this is unsatisfactory. Of course the reality that the audience knew must have informed the use of music in the plays, but this does not make the music functionally realistic: all it does is to recognize a known relation between drama and everyday life. We can say the same thing about the angelic

3

singing, for example, where it is the liturgical forms, with their texts, musical styles, and probably the plainsong tunes themselves, that characterize the heavenly celebrations. Although this may well have been realistic to some medieval people who expected Heaven to be like that, no-one will think it realistic in a twentieth-century sense.

Further thought should show that the examples cited by Stevens are not realistic in a modern sense, either. The 'Good' Gossips' song is not a real drinking song, for the text is immediately topical. No doubt it should be performed like a drinking song, quite differently from the accomplished singing of godly mortals or the professional singing of angelic music. The Towneley Second Shepherds' play shows us one of the implications of the music of God's chosen as I have explained it: an out-of-tune, unmusical singer is likely to be a bad character. So the lullaby sung by Mak is clearly a very unmusical and out-of-tune performance (*Towneley*, p. 131). The Chester Gossips, like Mak, must not be confused with the singers discussed earlier. Just as Mak is heard to be a discordant character, so the type of performance given by the Gossips characterizes them as tippling world-lovers.

The music for Herod is a slightly different case, for it must certainly be professional minstrelsy. The quality of performance is not in question. The music proper to a monarch's earthly power and pretensions was the loud, showy ceremonial music of a shawms-and-trumpet band, the standard loud band of the late Middle Ages and still in use in the seventeenth century. Any townsman watching a mystery play, and most countrymen, too, would have witnessed the reception of some important person into a town, and would have heard the ceremonial shawms-and-trumpet music of the town waits (professional musicians maintained by the town). But the music for Herod, again, although informed by actual usage, could hardly be realistic in its primary intention: for there would be little point in such realism when very few of those watching, if any, had actually attended a royal audience (*Chester*, p. 162; 'N-Town', p. 174) or a royal banquet ('N-Town', p. 176).

These two examples use marginally different means to define their own character – style of music and of performance in one case, style of music and instrumentation in the other – and yet they have a common function in the plays. Both are *representational*, just as the other types of music are, telling us the characters of the particular *dramatis personae* to whom the music is attached.

To explain this second representational use of music, we must return to the Boethian cosmology. Boethius's third category of music was *musica instrumentalis*, the music of human voices and instruments. This caused much thought in the Middle Ages, and was found to need further classification. It formed, as it were, the bottom end of a vertical line from Heaven to Earth of which the music of Divine Order was the top end. The problem was that its actual manifestations here on Earth were often quite at odds with their philosophical explanation. However much minstrelsy and singing might be seen ideally as a *speculum* of Divine Order, the observable fact was that a large number of musicians were the vicious and despicable dregs of society, people who could not easily be seen as imitators of the angelic minstrelsy. In order to reconcile cosmological theory and social fact attempts were made to see secular musicians as socially and morally classifiable: of these attempts, Thomas of Chabham's is perhaps the best known (Tydeman, pp. 187f). But there was also a body of opinion that refused this reconciliation and saw only minstrelsy's undoubted connection with prostitution, petty theft, and vice of all kinds. This second view is the thinking behind the use of music by the vices in the morality plays and by the ungodly characters in the mystery plays.

A second set of functions, first described by Dutka[2] and defined by her as functions that help to further the dramatic action, may be called 'structural'. Music often appears at the entrance of a new character or re-entrance of a character previously seen, the music here helping to focus our attention on the entrance itself. The precise definition of this function depends on the type of staging involved, however: for example, where a character disappears from the audience's sight in a processional pageant-staged play, he may well only move to one side of the acting area in a place-and-scaffold production. In the latter case, the music will serve to re-focus the audience's attention on a different part of the playing area when that character 'returns' for a new scene. In either case, the music helps a smooth transition from the end of one scene to the beginning of another. Similarly, music often occurs at the exit of a character: again, this may be an actual exit or only a moving-away to another part of the acting area. In the wagon-staged drama, exit-music at the end of the play might start in the acting area and continue as part of the procession to the next station. This technique was probably useful also in performances not of the processional type. A good example would be the *Te Deum laudamus* sung at the end of the Towneley Judgement play (*Towneley*, p. 387), where the whole company must be removed from the acting area however the play is staged. In the N-Town Noah play this procession also allows the ark to be removed ('N-Town', p. 43).

Another function of music was to cover movement around the acting area. The songs sung by the shepherds on their way to and from Bethlehem have this function, and so does the angelic singing which in Chester Play X covers the flight into Egypt (*Chester*, p. 196). A function closely related to this last is to mark the passage of time. This can occur when no movement around the acting area is involved: in the Chester Noah play, music covers the forty days in which the flood rises (*Chester*, p. 53).

It is in the nature of the drama under consideration that all the situations just described normally come at the break between one scene and another. Indeed, these functions are important in a repertory in which neither proscenium curtain nor blackout is available. In Shepherds' plays, the singing of the shepherds themselves often defines the beginning and end of the adoration scene at the manger, and in the Chester Shepherds' play every major scene-division has music. A much simpler play in which this happens (although the structure is more rigorous) is York Play XLV, 'The Assumption of the Virgin': this play consists of 24 stanzas, with a dramatic structure in three sections of eight stanzas each.[3] There is music at both of the main scene-divisions.

It is difficult to know what is the relative importance of these various representational and structural functions. It is clear that when music appears it fulfills both a representational and a structural function: but on the other hand there are plenty of places where music apparently does not occur even though it would be both representationally appropriate and structurally useful. Why is there music at some suitable places and not at others? Much of the answer must lie in the relative wealth of the guilds mounting the plays, and the circumstances in which the drama was re-hearsed and presented. Music was always an expensive commodity, and we should not assume that every guild mounting a play in which music was appropriate could or would afford it. Besides, the musical resources of even a major town were limited, and must often have been available only to the guild that asked first or offered the highest fee. At Coventry, the Smiths' Company made all four of the waits members in 1481, together with their wives, in order to make sure of the waits' professional services in their play (*REED Coventry*, p. 64). Choristers and singing-men would be in short supply, too, for even a large cathedral establishment could not maintain its sung services properly if its choir were greatly depleted by rehearsals and performances of the plays. At Chester, it is clear that very few singing-men were involved in any one production of the plays; and it seems very likely that in 1567 the Smiths' Guild was unable to hire a group of choristers, as it had done in previous years, because the boys were singing in the Painters' play.[4]

This uncertain and probably fluctuating situation is reflected in the sur-viving texts. In the case of the Chester plays, which exist in five sources (see Peter Meredith's discussion below, pp. 17ff.), we can see that the different manuscripts transmit different versions of what music the plays required. The greatest variation is in Play II: Manuscript B gives directions for minstrelsy in six places, but if that source had not survived we should have known only of the five places in Manuscript Hm; if that source, too, had been lost, we should have relied on Manuscripts A and R, which show only four places where minstrelsy was required; and without any of those manuscripts, looking at Manuscript H would not have told us of any

6

minstrelsy at all in that play. All other mystery cycles survive in unique sources, and we have no reason to think that any of those texts transmits a version with the fullest possible musical participation. Indeed, the laws of chance tell us that this is likely *not* to be the case. To put it positively, we may assume that when the surviving plays were put into production they are likely to have used music in some places where neither dialogue nor stage directions call for it in the existing copies.

To some extent we can help ourselves in this matter by reference to other types of evidence. Banns (proclamation or prologue of a play) survive for the N-Town and Chester plays, and from the Chester banns we learn that the Doomsday play included a piece of music – 'Venite bene-dicti' – that we should not otherwise know occurred in the play. But in other respects the banns are not very useful: for although they must presumably tell us what were considered to be audience-drawers in the plays, we have no means of knowing the precise reasons for the selection of these particular items. Was the angelic *Gloria* – mentioned in both sets of banns – a much more spectacular performance than angelic music in other plays, or did other factors make certain items mentioned in the banns for some reason specially important?

Of more help, although at this stage still largely to be explored, are the various account-books of the guilds mounting the mystery plays, gradually being published in the *REED* volumes. The account-books lead us to the conclusion that the musicians concerned generally supplied the music from their own musical resources. This is what we should expect, for the guilds, having no musical expertise to draw on, relied on professional musicians to provide appropriate music at the required places in the plays. In the case of instrumental music, the minstrels drew on a memorized repertory: there being no text involved, no one other than the minstrels concerned apparently had an interest in the piece to be performed. This explains why no title ever appears for instrumental music in the play-texts. The case of singers is a little different. All singers must be coached in their music and, for angelic music at least, professional singers must actually be supplied for the purpose. The Chester account-books contain payments for meeting the Master of the Choristers, the Precentor ('Mr Chanter'), or some other 'clerk' at an early stage of the preparations, eventually followed by pay-ments to singers. At these preliminary meetings the guilds presumably stated precisely what they wanted – what sort of music and where in the play, what sort of text, any accompaniment, and so on. On their side, the musical organisers must have agreed to supply singers, to rehearse and perform the music using their own music-books. There are indications that they sometimes composed new music for the purpose: admittedly a pay-ment to a professional musician 'for songes' (*REED Chester*, pp. 67 and 91) does not necessarily mean new compositions, but there are items in the

Coventry accounts showing that music was composed and copied (*REED Coventry*, pp. 223, 237 and 249), and there is other evidence to be discussed below.

On the matter of performance, too, the accounts give some information. Medieval iconography would suggest to us that such episodes from the cosmic story as the Assumption of the Virgin would be accompanied by a host of different types of musical instrument, either playing purely instrumental music or accompanying angelic singers. This is however contradicted by items in both the Chester and Coventry accounts, where it is clear that local professional singers were accompanied by an organist playing regals.[5] While this may seem surprising in view of the iconography of the time, it is in fact what we should expect from the way in which musicians then worked. Throughout the Middle Ages minstrelsy was performed according to an aural tradition, a minstrel being taught his craft without the aid of written music and performing from memory in the same way. This tradition is so unlike that of the church-trained singer and organist, who always performed from written music even when singing plainsong, that there can be no possibility – in England, at least until well into the sixteenth century – of the two traditions coming together in performance. The difficulties would be roughly those experienced by classically-trained instrumentalists and jazz musicians working together at the present time: the whole way of thought is different. We may therefore assume that in all but the latest mystery plays minstrels and church musicians performed separately, even when required in the same play.[6] It follows that in fifteenth-century plays angelic singing was accompanied by an organ of some type, played by a church musician. In the N-Town stage direction that requires the singing of angels to the accompaniment of 'organa', therefore, we can assume the obvious translation of 'organs' (i.e. a single instrument) rather than the equally-possible 'instruments':[7]

> *Et hic assendent in celum cantantibus organis ¶ Assumpta es Maria in celum.*
> ('N-Town', p. 373)
> (And here they will go up to Heaven with the music of *organa*: 'You, Mary, are taken up into Heaven'.)

Notated music survives in the texts of the York, Coventry, and Chester plays. Of these the oldest is the manuscript of the York plays, which has been dated from the period between 1463 and 1477 (Beadle and Meredith, p. 55). Play XLV, 'The Assumption of the Virgin', belongs to this main compilation, so that the copying of the music, too, can be assigned to this period. At three points in the play, during St Thomas's vision of the Assumption of Our Lady, angelic music is heard. Of the three texts (all in Latin) only one can be identified as a liturgical text.[8] Each piece is for two voices, and is presumably to be sung by the twelve angels (or by some of them) specified by the text. At the end of the play are alternative settings of the same three texts: these are copied in the same hand as the others, and must also date from the time of the main compilation of the manuscript, 1463–77. There is evidence that all six pieces were composed by the same man, and that he worked in something of a hurry, for there is considerable interchange of musical material between the pieces and some rather strange miscalculations of a type that composers can eliminate on reflection. The alternative versions, although written for the same type of voice, are generally longer and in all cases more difficult than the settings in the body of the text. The singers were presumably choristers from the Minster, though no relevant records survive: but while the first versions would require highly-trained boy singers, the alternative versions can only have been sung by the very ablest choristers.

There are several songs in the two plays surviving from the otherwise lost Coventry plays, but only in the Shearmen and Tailors' play of the Nativity and Massacre of the Innocents is there any musical notation. When Sharp published the text of this play he included a quasi-facsimile of the music, engraved by his illustrator, David Jee: and as the manuscript was subsequently destroyed in a fire at the Birmingham Free Library in 1879, Sharp's edition and Jee's engraving are the only surviving remains of this play and its music. The play text was a revised version made in 1534, but the songs were apparently added to the end of the play in 1591. However, there is evidence that at least one of the two songs was already used in performance by 1534, and the musical style of both songs is consistent with a date in the 1530s. The first song is that sung by the shepherds as they go to Bethlehem to adore the Child. Here, as in other shepherds' plays, their music defines the beginning of the adoration scene and also covers the journey as they walk to Bethlehem. Their song 'As I out rode this enderes night', with its second verse 'Doune from heaven', is a splendid song that deserves to be better known. The second song is the famous lullaby, the so-called 'Coventry carol', sung by the mothers of the Innocents before the massacre. An interesting feature of this song – disguised by its general use at Christmas-time in a spurious four-part version, and by the fact that it is rarely used in the drama itself – is that it was sung by three men (alto, tenor, and bass) impersonating women. The stage direction at the mothers' entry is quite explicit – *Here the wemen cum in wythe there chyldur syngyng them* . . . (*Coventry*, p. 29) – so there is no doubt that the singers played the women's roles. The voice-types are the same as those of the shepherds. Indeed, the two sets of roles could easily be played by the same singers: almost thirty minutes' drama separates the final exit of the shepherds and the entry of the women with the Innocents. This leaves ample time for the necessary costume-change, and it would be surprising if the guild did not double the roles.

No other sources are known for either the York pieces or those in the Coventry play. We may take this as *prima facie* evidence that music written into a play text is likely to be unavailable elsewhere, and composed especially for the play concerned; and that it is unlikely to be found in any normal (non-dramatic) musical source. The evidence is however negative, and it will be as well to continue the search for other sources of all these pieces. The surviving music in the Chester cycle, a mere fragment in the Nativity play (*Chester*, p. 605), is a rather different case. Only one manuscript includes it, and that is the latest of the five sources (manuscript H, dating from 1607). The text underlaid to the single line of music, 'Gloria in excelsis deo', is incomplete, for the stage direction and the dialogue (*Chester*, pp. 141–4) show that the angels sing to the shepherds the complete text given in Luke 2, v. 14 (but with 'excelsis' for the gospel's 'altissimis', the former being the liturgical version), which adds 'et in terra pax hominibus bonae voluntatis'. We may assume, therefore, that the musical line is merely an *incipit*. The text appears in the liturgy most importantly as the verse to the first responsory at Mattins on Christmas Day. The Chester music does not seem to be based on the chant of this item, nor to work contrapuntally with it. The line does seem, on the other hand, to be the opening point of a polyphonic setting (i.e. part music) such as many composers wrote in the mid-sixteenth century: but I have not been able to identify this setting.

In this chapter I have had two main aims: to discuss the broad outlines of a rationale for the use of music in the mystery plays and to review the main types of evidence to which we look for information about the musical details of production. The broad outlines can be identified in drama dating from later than the main period of the mystery plays. John Bale's use of 'heavenly' singing in *God's Promises* – almost certainly accompanied by an organ in the Kilkenny production of 1553[9] – is recognizably that of the mystery plays, whatever the differences in other respects; and Shakespeare's classic exposition of Boethian cosmology in *The Merchant of Venice* expresses a view that still had currency in the early seventeenth century:

> There's not the smallest orb that thou behold'st
> But in his motion like an angel sings,
> Still quiring to the young-ey'd cherubins;
> Such harmony is in immortal souls,
> But whilst this muddy vesture of decay
> Doth grossly close it in, we cannot hear it.
>   (V. i. 60–65)

On the other hand, these broad principles need to be refined. I have already stated that the morality plays used music in a representational way that is relatively rare in the mystery plays; and in saints' plays the use of music was different again. We must, then, take into account the precise type of play concerned. But even in biblical plays the situation may not be simple in respect of music. The Shrewsbury Fragments, for example, are known to be liturgically-based plays from Lichfield Cathedral, and the implications of this are important for the music. Here we have the musical establishment of a cathedral, able to devote all its resources to an event which is part of the full-time occupation of those acting and singing, carried out in its normal location: this is very different from the performance of those few singers that could be spared, helping in a craft play acted out of doors by men who were not professionally concerned with liturgy. We cannot, then, use the Shrewsbury plays as evidence for *civic* performances, and the same is true of other biblical plays that seem to be ecclesiastical, rather than civic, in origin: notably the Bodley *Burial* and *Resurrection* plays (*Digby*, pp. 190ff). Specifically, the Shrewsbury plays and the Bodley *Resurrection* cannot be used to show that mortal characters sang polyphony in civic plays during the fifteenth century.

Another necessary refinement concerns chronology and regional location. In the 1560s music for the Coventry Drapers' play was regularly supplied by James Hewet, one of the town waits, among others (*REED Coventry*, passim). Some of his colleagues sang at Holy Trinity Church, so Hewet may have been a church-trained organist, although a civic instrumentalist by profession. This situation could not have occurred in the fifteenth century, when only a church musician could have taken charge of the music. The changed circumstances show themselves, too, in the part-songs composed for mortal characters in the Shearmen and Tailors' play, something else that we could not look for in fifteenth-century productions. As for differences due to regional locality, we need only remind ourselves, as an example, that while the Coventry Drapers paid a secular musician for their music the guilds at Chester continued to hire musicians from the cathedral.

It will be seen that our potential knowledge of production details partly depends on our understanding of the use of music generally in early English drama. As will be clear from earlier parts of this chapter, the evidence for production details is often difficult to interpret: none of it was designed to give vital information to twentieth-century producers. This is not the place to discuss a subject that is at best highly speculative, but a specific problem, taken merely as an example, may help to show the nature of our difficulty. In the Coventry Shearmen and Tailors' play, Herod retires to rest, commanding the music of viols and trumpets from his minstrels (*Coventry*, p. 19). We may assume that music is heard. The trumpets may well have been a loud band of the type that I have previously

11

mentioned, but viols are not an obvious choice for the representation of Herod. I have said that Herod's music must have been clearly distinguishable, by style and instrumentation, from 'heavenly' minstrelsy. The loud band allows this, because the weight of late medieval iconographical evidence shows that the instrumental music of Divine Order was primarily the soft indoor music of strings and organs. I have mentioned organs before, but there is only one instance of stringed instruments being specified in a fifteenth-century mystery play:

> *hic discendet angelus ludentibus citharis* . . .
> ('N-Town', p. 358)
> (Here the angel will descend to the playing of harps . . .)

But if the soft minstrelsy of Heaven is always to be distinguished from the loud ceremonial music of Herod, what of Herod's viols in the Coventry play? It is hardly likely that viols (though bowed, not plucked) would fail to bring Heaven to mind if that tradition were still strong. Is the Coventry example, then, the result of a sixteenth-century breakdown of understanding of the established practice, and is this deviation peculiar to Coventry? Or are the viols part of an older – and perhaps widely-understood – tradition that has somehow failed to come to our notice?

We need not try to justify answers at this stage. My own belief is that the Coventry Herod's viols are indeed a sixteenth-century deviation, perhaps part of an attempt to bring the play up-to-date. Whether they are peculiar to Coventry or not we cannot say, since no relevant evidence from elsewhere is known to exist. The important point is that these questions have to be asked in any attempt to assess the possible interpretations of evidence that fails to give a clear answer. Research on the music of the plays may well concern itself very much in the next few years with assessing the details of the evidence in this way.

Scribes, texts and performance

Peter Meredith

The importance of manuscript evidence for an understanding of late medieval drama has been clear at least since W. W. Greg's pioneering work on the English mystery plays at the beginning of this century.[1] Yet despite an awareness of the basic importance of this kind of study, much scholarly discussion (and, incredibly it seems, even some editing) has with certain notable exceptions proceeded with only a nod in the direction of the manuscript. The appearance of facsimiles of the major manuscripts has encouraged, and should further encourage, those interested to go back to the manuscript to find out what the scribes were doing.[2] Even though the interpretation of manuscript evidence is a complex matter and often ends only in speculation about what the scribe intended, nevertheless it is essential that it should be attempted if only to establish the kinds of basic question that need to be asked about the nature of the text and its relationship with performance.

It has, for example, been usual to talk about stage directions using the term in the same way as for a modern play. But are the 'stage directions' of medieval plays really this kind of thing? Who wrote them, for instance? The author? A scribe who happened to see a performance; a scribe with the Bible or one with an ideal performance in his mind? A producer (if the word is meaningful in a medieval English context), or a prompter? The answer is, of course, that it could have been any of these, or indeed all of them. Few texts have stage directions all of one kind or of one date.

It is now unfashionable to believe that one can establish an authoritative text of a medieval work of literature. If this is true of a non-dramatic work, it is much more so of a play. The play may not merely be going through the hands of scribes but through the mouths of actors and the mill of production. What do we know of the treatment of the text of a civic play in England in the later Middle Ages? There is almost an unspoken acceptance of a kind of hierarchy of texts: the *Register*, the authoritative full copy of the whole cycle, kept by the town or city; the *original*, the copy of the individual pageant held by the craft or guild; the *parcels*, the parts copied

13

out and used by the craft members in learning their parts. If this is so (and certainly these three types of text did exist) then the chances of a wide variety of texts developing are enormous; the *parcels* could be altered and annotated in the course of production; these changes might or might not reach the *original* (itself possibly annotated); this in turn might or might not affect the *Register*.

But do we know what the actual relationship was between these types of text? Where did the Register come from? Is it the author's text, perhaps at some remove from the earliest form of the Corpus Christi cycle? Or is it merely the sum of its parts, a registering of already existing craft pageants? And what is the status of the annotations? It has been customary to label most of these with some such phrase as 'by a later hand' thereby denying them any authority. But what if they are corrections or additions from the craft guild's own copy? A play that lasts nearly two hundred years is not likely to remain static; these are not author's but they may well be owner's revisions and as such perhaps equally worth a place in the text. It is worth remembering that the texts that we possess (none earlier than the second half of the fifteenth century and some very much later) almost certainly contain many annotations 'by a later hand', absorbed into the text and now indistinguishable from the rest of it.

From what I have already said it will be clear that going back to the manuscript also means going back to the records of the place where the play was performed. It is not possible to answer questions about the use of a text without referring constantly to city and guild records. The text of a play is only one (though an important one) amongst a number of pieces of evidence for the functioning of the play in performance. This does not entirely differentiate a play from, say, a sermon, which has a similar kind of context; or even from a poem orally delivered, but for a play the context – the organisation, setting, costumes, properties, style of acting – is more important and more integral to the text than it is for either of these others. Fortunately through the work of the Malone Society and *Records of Early English Drama* the records are becoming more easily accessible and the published versions more dependable.[3]

Though the records are an essential part of establishing a context for the play, they cannot answer all the questions. Sometimes this is because of the difficulty of attaching a manuscript to a place; sometimes because of loss. It is important to remember that consecutive evidence from year to year, for guild or city, is the exception rather than the rule. Of all the craft guilds of York, only the Mercers' provides anything like continuous records from the early fifteenth century to the late sixteenth century, and even in these there are numerous gaps.

I have up to now been talking in general terms about the texts and the records of the plays but what is most striking about the major cycles of mystery plays, given that the sources of their subject matter were the same, is their variety. This is nowhere more true than in their manuscripts and it is to an individual consideration of three groups of these that I now wish to turn.

York – British Library Additional MS 35290

The manuscript of the York play – the *Ludus Corporis Cristi* or Corpus Christi play – is in some ways the easiest to deal with since its provenance, its date, its scribes, the reasons for its compilation and its owners are all to some extent known. It contains the texts of forty-eight of the craft pageants. Space has been left specifically for two others, the Vintners' and the Ironmongers', but neither was registered. In the case of the Vintners' this is particularly unfortunate since it was the only play on the subject of the Marriage at Cana in the English mystery cycles. The manuscript was written in the late 1460's or 1470's in York, probably by local scribes. That they were local is an assumption, not a proven fact. 'Registering' was however the normal process by which a document of importance to the City was copied into one of its large books, called therefore *registers*, and it is difficult to imagine the City Council going outside the ranks of its own perfectly adequate clerks for the registering of something so entirely a City matter as the play. Moreover the style of lay-out and script is very much the kind of work that the better of the City's clerks produced elsewhere in the City records – a normally neat but workaday script, not elaborately laid out or decorated. The local knowledge implied in the English craft names perhaps also points to a City scribe.

The Register – and of all the manuscripts of the plays the York one most deserves the name – was almost certainly written to provide the City with a quick and accurate reference book for checking the performances of the play and noting changes of craft responsibility. In this it replaced the *Ordo Paginarum* which was a brief description of each of fifty-one pageants, originally written in 1415 by the Common Clerk Roger Burton, but much altered. Until the writing of the Register this seems to have been the only check that the City had on the contents of the pageants.

The first mention of the Register in the City records is in 1527 when 2s 4d was provided as expenses for Thomas Clerke 'deputato communis Clerici custodiendum Registrum' ('deputy of the Common Clerk for keeping the Register'). This 'keeping of the Register' is the only real clue to the use to which the manuscript was later put, and the phrase recurs fairly regularly in the station lists from 1538 onwards in conjunction with the place for the Common Clerk at the first station opposite Holy Trinity priory gates – 'the ffyrst place at Trenytie yaites where as the Comon Clerke kepys the

15

Registre' (*REED York*, p. 263). The station lists recorded the places where the pageants were to stop to perform, and also the payments made for the privilege of having a station at one's door. The place for the Common Clerk, set aside officially and costing nothing, appears first in the station list of 1501. Certainly from that time on the Common Clerk or his deputy was expected to sit with the Register at the point where the pageants first turned into the pageant route to perform. Why? I have already suggested that the City kept a check on the pageants and it seems that for some reason in the 1460s and 1470s they decided to make it possible not just generally to check on the contents but precisely to check the text; the pageants in the Register could be compared word for word as the actors spoke. This fits with the concern for 'þe honour of þe Citie and Worship of þe saide Craftes' that underlies the 1476 ordinance regarding the players in the Corpus Christi play (*REED York*, p. 109).

It is clear that the Register was also kept up to date by occasional comparison with the craft-guilds' own copies. Some alterations, for example those in the Shipwrights' pageant, could hardly have been made on the spot at the first station. Likewise the extensive addition to the Glovers' pageant seems more likely to have come from a comparison of Register and craft copy. It is possible that this kind of checking is referred to in the attempt made by the City to bring in the unregistered pageants in 1567: '[the pageant of] the Cappers to be examined with the Register & reformed' (*REED York*, p. 351).

The manuscript of the York play is then a late-fifteenth-century official civic document, compiled for the purpose of control over the activities of the crafts in their Corpus Christi pageants. Written apparently by local scribes, it was annotated in their official capacities by the Common Clerks or their deputies, often during the performance of the play at the first station, or corrected by them from the craft copies. It is last heard of in the City's hands when it was to be sent for correction to the Archbishop and Dean of York in 1579 for a projected performance that never took place (*REED York*, p. 390).

York – the Sykes Manuscript (York City Archives)[4]

Only one copy of an *original* survives from York: 'The Incredulity of Thomas'. Considering that it was the Scriveners' own copy of their pageant, it is a surprisingly undistinguished booklet. It consists of four parchment leaves enclosed within a folder of parchment. It dates from the first half of the sixteenth century and is therefore later than the Register. It differs from the text of the Register in innumerable minor ways and also in the omission of one line and the inclusion of another. (*York* lines 27–8 missing

16

in Sykes; Sykes 1.181 missing in Register). These differences show that texts could already have been faulty when copied into the Register, and that new faults (as well as revisions) would continue to appear in the craft copies. By the late fifteenth century the *original* was very unlikely still to be the original.

Despite the differences that exist between the two texts there are no annotations to this effect in the Register. This could mean that the Scriveners' pageant was no longer being performed during the period when the Common Clerks were keeping the Register, but the existence of the Sykes manuscript makes this unlikely. It is more likely to be an indication that the Common Clerks were not always as vigilant in their checking or that by the end of a long day attention began to wander. The Sykes manuscript is also devoid of annotation so that unfortunately it gives no idea of how production notes or alterations might have reached the official copies of the play.

No *parcels* survive from York (nor from any other of the major plays in England), nor is there any reference to them in the records.

Chester – Huntington Library MS 2; BL MS Additional 10305; BL MS Harley 2013; Bodleian Library MS Bodley 175; BL MS Harley 2124

I have chosen to deal with Chester next since it is the only English mystery play besides York which survives in something like its entirety (the cycle consists of 24/25 pageants) and which is closely and certainly associated with a particular city. Even from the list of manuscripts, however, one marked difference will be immediately apparent: York survives in a unique City copy, Chester survives in five copies, none associated with the City authorities. Moreover the date of the York text is well within the period of the performance of the play (late fourteenth century to 1569), whereas all the Chester manuscripts date from some time after the last recorded performance in 1575: Huntington, 1591; Additional, 1592; Harley 2013, 1600; Bodley, 1604; and Harley 2124, 1607. It is also worth noting that though in York there are signs of a desire to renew the performance of the play after 1569 despite ecclesiastical opposition, there is no sign in Chester of any similar desire; indeed the Chester Coopers' company seems to have been selling off its pageant carriage wheels in the year after what later turned out to be the last performance (*REED Chester*, p. 117). Chester, however, had its Midsummer Show to replace the lost play; York had almost nothing.

The main question which arises about these manuscripts is why they were written. Chester is sharply distinct from York in one way especially: there was an enormous amount of antiquarian activity in the City in the late sixteenth and early seventeenth centuries. Not only are there the

Mayors' lists and the Rogers' Breviary recording dates and describing City activities, but there were the four Randle Holmes copying and transcribing City and guild records.[5] To some extent no doubt this activity sprang from the practical purpose of recording the past for such legal reasons as the settling of disputes, but in the main it seems likely that all the play texts are antiquarian copies made to preserve or to recall ancient City ceremonial. They were certainly not made as acting or production copies.

They were in three cases, however, copied out by the kind of men who at an earlier date might well have been called upon to provide acting copies for the companies. George Bellin, in particular, was clerk to the Coopers' company as well as the scribe of Additional 10305 and Harley 2013; William Bedford was later clerk to the Brewers' and also scribe of Bodley 175. We might therefore expect a format and a mode of copying not dissimilar from that of the Sykes Manuscript or the York Register, but, on the other hand, one which may conceal later marginal additions. Huntington and Harley 2124 are somewhat different. The former was written by Edward Gregory, who describes himself as 'scholler at Bunburye', a small town near Chester, and the latter was written partly by James Miller, probably a minor canon of Chester Cathedral. It is this last manuscript that is different in format as well as in text from the others. It provides unique sections of text, links two elsewhere distinct pageants together, has 'stage directions' in Latin, a number of Biblical texts in the margin and a carefully prepared lay-out.

A further question in relation to the manuscripts is what they were copied from. Was there a *Register* at Chester? Were it not for a single reference in the records, the answer might well have been: apparently not. Though the term used there is 'the originall booke of the whydson plaies' (*REED Chester*, p. 80), there is no doubt that it was the City's book and very little that it was a complete text of the cycle. It is therefore possible that the extant texts go back to a City Register (though it should not be forgotten – bearing the York Register in mind – that that copy might well retain the individual idiosyncracies of the craft *originals*), or also possible that they go back to a set of craft *originals*.

The mention of craft *originals* and of *parcels* copied from them is common in the Chester records, and two additional pieces of evidence arise from these references: first, some confirmation that the *parcels* were indeed parts for the actors (*REED Chester*, pp. 66 and 95); and secondly, that the *original* was in some way used at the performance at Whitsun. Its most likely use was as a prompt book, but bearing the York Common Clerks in mind it is just possible that through 'the Reygenall beyrer' ('the person who carried the *original*', *REED Chester*, p. 50) or 'him that Rydeth ('reads') the orrygynall' (*REED Chester*, p. 83) the companies were keeping an eye on their own actors' treatment of the text.

Chester – National Library of Wales MS Peniarth 399; Chester Coopers' Company MS

Besides the five complete texts of the plays there are also two surviving *originals*: the Antichrist pageant (Peniarth 399) of the early sixteenth century, and the Coopers' Trial and Flagellation pageant of 1599. The latter clearly springs from the desire of the company to 'register' its own pageant and like the manuscripts of the whole cycle it is not an acting copy. It was written by George Bellin. The Antichrist pageant on the other hand dates from the period of the production of the plays, though there is little in the way of annotation beyond the altering of a few words.

Though there is a good deal of evidence from Chester for the use of the *originals* there is none for the use of the City's copy of the plays.

N-Town – BL MS Cotton Vespasian D VIII[6]

The N-Town plays are very different from those of York and Chester. Though they contain elements of a cycle – such as the Banns and many individual pageants – they also contain complete plays which were never part of a cycle. Furthermore, they are not associated with any one place or any one time of the year, and as evidence for their performance there is only the manuscript itself. There is also no sign that they were ever the possessions of crafts or companies.

Both York and Chester contain a series of separate pageants – a typical mystery play cycle; what we have in the N-Town manuscript is a miscellaneous collection of often disparate plays. There are a number of individual pageants, but there is also a composite play on the early life of Mary and a two-part Passion play. Unfortunately, these two forms of play, unique in England, have been altered and adapted by the main scribe of the manuscript to fit with the cycle form which he has attempted to impose on the whole manuscript. It is not entirely clear what he had in mind, but he seems to have wanted completeness and continuity while at the same time leaving the possibility open of disconnecting (and perhaps performing separately) some of the parts.

His desire for completeness may be related to the purpose of the manuscript. It has been suggested that it was, like *The Castle of Perseverance*, the property of a touring company. This seems to me in a high degree unlikely. There is no sign of a touring company of the later Middle Ages in England that could have put on *The Castle of Perseverance* (see below, pp. 103–4) let alone tackled the complexities of staging the N-Town plays. It could, on the other hand, have been intended as a touring *manuscript*. There is growing evidence in East Anglia for the banding together of small towns into groups for the performance of plays, but no evidence so far of where the texts came from. It is at least possible that the pageant part of the N-Town plays was prepared as a text for borrowing, and therefore one which would be played in a variety of places – hence the 'N-Town' of the Banns:

> A sunday next yf þat we may   *On*
> At vj of þe belle we gynne oure play
> In N. Town wherfore we pray
> That God now be ʒoure spede.
> ('N-Town', p. 16)

Besides which, performance by a group of towns is one which requires advertisement and perhaps travelling *vexillatores* ('proclaimers/announcers of the play'), such as those of the N.-Town Banns, to announce the performance.

The idea of a manuscript to be borrowed might also explain the addition and adaptation that has extended the pageant cycle, and the apparently detachable parts. Any prospective 'producer' could be shown on the one hand the possible range of material, and on the other, that if there were not the resources to produce the whole, that sections could be taken out of it and produced separately. There is only one sign in the manuscript itself that this was done, and it is not along the lines apparently suggested by the main scribe. A section in the latter part of the Passion plays is marked at the beginning *Incipit hic* ('Begin here'; f. 189 'N-Town', p. 312) and at the end *finem jᵃ die* ('end of first day'; f. 196 'N-Town', p. 327)). It isolates the setting of the watch, the latter part of the Harrowing of Hell, the Resurrection, and the return of the soldiers to Pilate, and it implies at least a two-day play. The scribe seems to have intended that the early life of Mary, once a separate play, could still be detached – if his alternative ending on f. 73v-f. 74 ('N-Town', pp. 120–1) is intended as a rounding-off and an avoidance of continuity with the next pageant, as it seems to be.

Using terms like *Register* and *original* in a discussion of the N-Town manuscript is inappropriate because of their implications of civic organisation. The matters that the N-Town manuscript raises are related to revision – turning a heterogeneous collection of plays into a homogeneous whole; and to the nature of the earlier texts which were basic material for this. The Assumption pageant in N-Town, for example, was a separate booklet before it was bound into the composite manuscript. The first part of the Passion play is also a booklet, of a somewhat more complex kind, but equally having had an existence of its own before being incorporated into the larger manuscript. The Assumption has been little touched by the main scribe, just enough to bring it into line with the appearance of the rest of the manuscript.[7] The first part of the Passion play, on the other hand, has been revised and adapted; mainly, it seems, to include material mentioned in the Banns (and therefore part of the earlier pageant series though not previously part of the Passion play) but also perhaps to make it more all-inclusive. The 'Life of Mary' play has been adapted somewhat differently. In this case the scribe has copied out the play afresh, but where it overlapped with material from the pageant series (mainly at the Betrothal of Mary) he has blended it and produced a composite version. At the end of the Mary play he blended and even possibly re-wrote in order to link it up with the following pageant material.

We have then in N-Town a situation quite different from that of the other manuscripts. There we have scribes doing their best, at York to produce texts acceptable to the City or craft, which were accurate records of what was being performed, at Chester antiquarian copies of past ceremonial. In N-Town we have a scribe adapting, blending and revising to produce an all-inclusive play apparently adequate to anyone's needs.

The diversity which the manuscripts show in their background and make-up is reflected in the nature and source of the information which they provide about performance. At York it is the comments of the Common Clerks and their deputies, in particular John Clerke, deputy from the 1530s until the end of the plays, that provide the information.[8] Their comments are of a number of different kinds. There are the indications of material missing on a large scale, and there are the *hic caret* ('here something is missing') references which could mean anything from a word to a complete speech. These are important for signs of revision in the pageants, but frustrating because they often tell us no more. Occasionally the whole situation is made clear, as in the stanza added to the Cardmarkers' pageant (ff. 7 and 9v; *York Facsimile* p. 15); occasionally we are given an *incipit*:

Alas that I was borne
dixit prima anima mala & ij[a] said the first evil soul, and the second
anima mala de nouo facta   evil soul – made new
   (f. 264; *York* p. 412)

This particular example (see plate 1) is interesting for two reasons: first because of the use of *dixit* ('said') instead of *dicit* ('says'), implying description rather than direction; and secondly, because the *incipit* happens to be the first line of what looks like an intrusive stanza spoken by one of the damned souls in the Towneley Last Judgement pageant, itself an expansion of the York one (*Towneley*, p. 367). This is not a conclusive argument for saying that we can reconstruct the missing speech, because the line is too commonplace, but it opens up an interesting possibility.

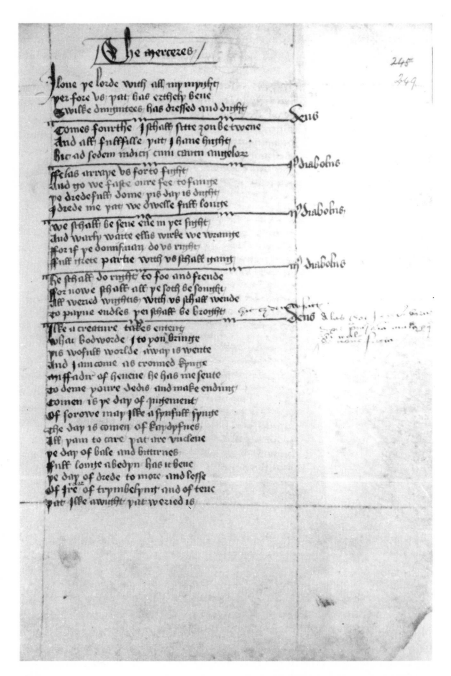

Plate 1: *Page from the Mercer's pageant at York, showing marginal annotations by John Clerke (British Library MS Additional 35290, f. 264).*

There are also the added 'stage directions'. These are important not usually for their content but because, being descriptions rather than directions, we can rely on the action actually having taken place. The indications of music however do considerably increase our understanding of performance. It is worth knowing for example that before Gabriel spoke the angelic greeting to Mary, he, or another angel, sang it (cf. p. 2 above): first (presumably) an *Ave Maria* ('Hail Mary') and then *Ne timeas Maria* ('Do not be afraid Mary'). When he speaks, therefore, his speeches are expansions of the sung pieces. Again at the Ascension the marginal notes show that Christ's rising was accompanied by angelic music, and interestingly enough here the music was changed in the course of the early sixteenth century from *Gloria in excelsys deo* to *Ascendo ad patrem meum* ('I ascend to my Father', f. 239, *York* p. 377). We are becoming used to the idea of revision of text: it is useful to have evidence that the choice of music could also change.

Momentary impressions of staging also come through sometimes in the marginal additions. The interpolated 'Oyes' of the messenger (?) in the Tilemakers' pageant summoning Christ to appear (f. 183v, *York* p. 300); the heel-clicking 'Lorde' of the soldiers in the Bowyers' and Fletchers' (f. 144, *York* p. 243), which they seem to have caught from the knights in the Tapiters' and Couchers' (f. 163, *York* p. 269), where there is an absolutely similar call and response; or the badly mistimed speech by the agonized Isaac in the Parchmenters' and Bookbinders' (f. 33v, *York* p. 95, between lines 165 and 166). The actor playing Isaac seems, on one occasion at least, to have come in with his line 'Why! fadir, will god þat I be slayne?' (l. 189) slightly 'revised' and twenty-four lines earlier.[9]

Perhaps most important of all as insights into the organisation of the performance are the indications given, mainly by Clerke, of the joining of pageants – what Richard Beadle has called 'playing in tandem' – which affect the Cardmakers' and Fullers', the Tilemakers' and Chandlers', and the Masons' and Goldsmiths' pageants.

If York provides a miscellany of suggestive details through the annotations of the Common Clerks and their deputies, the Chester manuscripts supply a wealth of direct but not always explicit information through the stage directions. Some are clear and revealing, like the description of the mechanics of the dove in the Harley 2124 version of 'Noah's Flood':

Tunc emittet columbam; et erit in nave aliam columbam ferens olivam in ore, quam dimittet aliquis ex malo per funem in manibus Noe.

('Then he shall send out a dove; and in the ship will be another dove carrying olive in its mouth, which someone shall let down by a cord from the mast into the hands of Noah'; *Chester* p. 464.)

Earlier in the same pageant Noah and his family are said to 'make a signe as though the ('they') wrought upon the shippe with divers instrumentes'

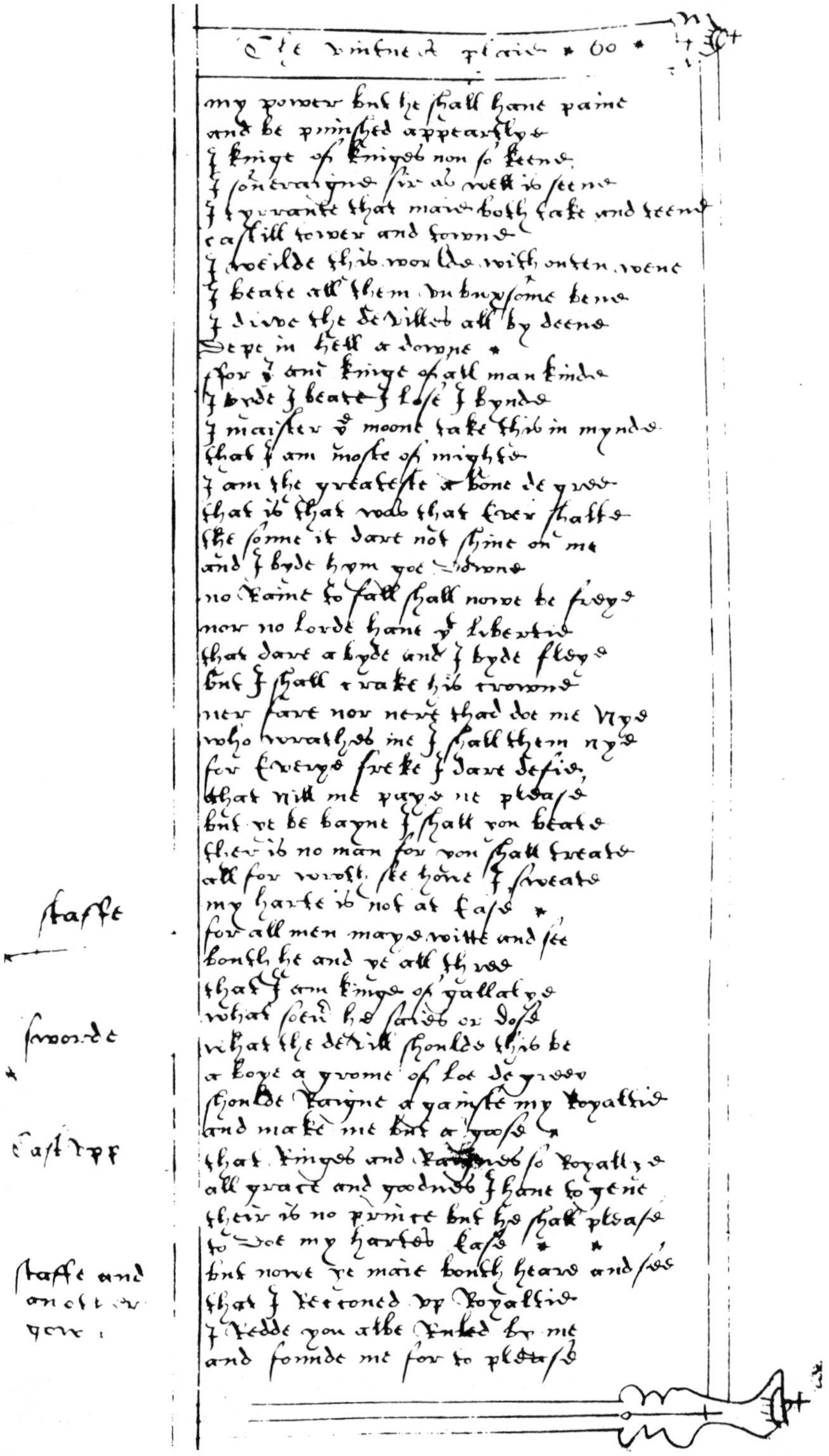

Plate 2: *Marginal directions for Herod's speech in the Vintners' pageant at Chester (British Library MS Additional 10305, f. 60).*

(*Chester* p. 47), clearly implying a pre-constructed ark. The phrase 'make a sign' (or in the case of the Latin directions, *faciet signum*) is something of a feature of the Chester plays. It covers actions of a very varied kind; from Moses cutting the tablets of the Law from the mountain (*Chester* p. 82), to the angel in the Purification pageant writing the word *virgo* back into Simeon's book (*Chester* p. 206). Herod too 'makes a sign': *Tunc faciet signum quasi morietur* ('Then he shall make a sign as though he were dying', *Chester* p. 201).

The positioning of the stage directions on the page varies from manuscript to manuscript, from pageant to pageant and from direction to direction.[10] One group, however, in all but Harley 2124, is placed in the left margin; what might reasonably perhaps be called the more casual side of the text. Because of the antiquarian nature of the manuscripts there is no difference in hand or script between these directions and the main text, but they bear all the signs of director's or actor's jottings (see plate 2.) They accompany the speeches of Herod in the Magi pageant (*Chester* pp. 163–74), and consist of the following: 'staffe, staffe, sworde, Cast vpp, staffe and an other gowne, a bill, caste downe þe sworde, breake a sworde, caste vp, caste vp, the boye and pigge when the kinges are gone, staffe, sworde, caste vp'.[11] If these do derive from the jottings of a director or actor, what do they mean? The first note of the series, 'staffe', occurs beside the line: 'Bien soies venues, royes gent' ('Welcome, noble kings', l. 157) at the moment when Herod first greets the three kings. The second, 'staffe' again, occurs at l. 197: 'For all men may wott and see', where Herod is controlling his anger and re-adopting his regal pose. This gives a definite clue to the use of the staff: an expression of Herod's regality, his staff of office. But where does he get it from? From the back of the pageant carriage? By his throne? And when does he put it down? It seems to me that we have here the typical situation for the 'conjuror's assistant'. When a piece of equipment is needed the assistant is there to provide it, and who more likely than the messenger to play the part. The pattern of the action then would be of a Herod wavering between frenzy and desperate regality being fed props by his messenger. This makes sense of the 'staffe and an other gowne' both as a symbolic donning of regality and as a viable piece of stage business.

There is then no trouble with the provision of props, but what does Herod do with them? With the staff there is no problem. He grasps it, and when his moment of regality is over he hands it (or throws it) back to his messenger. But 'Cast vpp'? Since he is holding a sword it must surely refer to that, and there seem to be two explanations of what he is doing. The dull one is that he is raising his arm in a rhetorical sweep; the other is that he actually throws the sword in the air. Either is possible. If the former is correct, then when he later 'casts down' his sword it is simply the gesture in reverse. He is then able to 'break the sword' that he has in his hand. After breaking the sword there are two 'caste vp's in quick succession, then towards the end of the pageant a further flurry of swordplay. This may be simply rhetorical flourishing, but there remains the possibility that Herod is almost juggling with the swords (there is clearly more than one), and that we are dealing with a whirling dervish rather than a frenzied orator.

When writing of one of the performers for the Painters', Salter says 'there would be no "goynge one the styltes" at the Whitsun plays' (p. 126). Would there also be no juggling with swords? I think we are in danger of being too sobersided about the plays and not allowing for the possibility that people with particular entertainment skills might well be encouraged to introduce them into the plays. There is a grisly delight in sword juggling skilfully performed which might well increase the horror of Herod rather than the comedy.

Whether we accept the broadly gesturing or the 'juggling' version of Herod the important thing to be aware of is that here we are given an extraordinary insight into the stage business of a pageant. Nowhere else do we come so close to an actual performance. It is worth noting that Balaak, though but a pale reflection of Herod, is given a similar style of acting if the stage directions are any guide: 'Florish, Caste vp, Sworde' (*Chester* pp. 83–4). And there is one further use of this kind of direction; in the Peniarth manuscript Antichrist himself is momentarily given a hint of the same style, and it begins to seem as though there is a Chester way of representing evil ranters. Especially interesting is that this direction, 'stafe' (lines 401 and 502), occurs only in the Peniarth MS, the Dyers' *original*. What other marginal directions did not find their way through to the five antiquarian manuscripts?

The N-Town plays are, as I have already suggested, very different from York and Chester. The manuscript is a composite one, made up of an incomplete pageant series and two diverse plays, a 'Life of Mary' play and a two-part Passion play. Here I want to consider how the main scribe of the manuscript blends the material of pageants and plays together to give an impression of continuity, and also to look at the possibilities of disentangling the blending to reveal the earlier forms of the plays. There is, regrettably, space here for only one sample of his methods – from the 'Life of Mary'.

The earlier 'Life of Mary' play contains no mention of the episode of Joseph's Trouble about Mary (in 'N-Town' called 'Joseph's Return') according to the description which *Contemplacio*, the expositor or commentator of the play, gives of the play's contents ('N-Town', pp. 62–3, 71 and 81–2). From the Banns, on the other hand, which gave the contents of the pageant series, it is clear that there was a pageant on this subject in that series. Such a pageant appears in the manuscript ('N-Town', pp. 109–15)

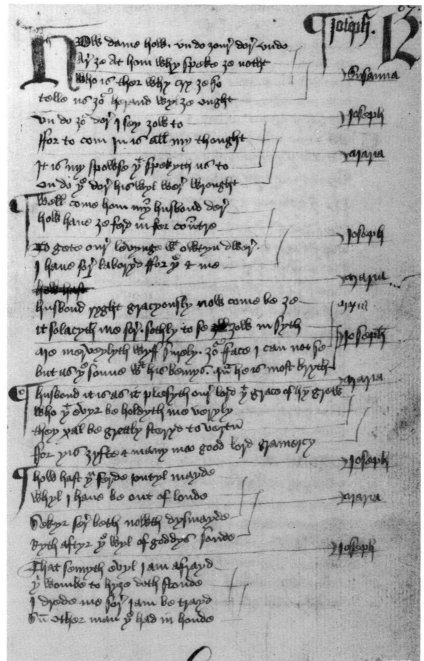

Plate 3: *Opening of 'Joseph's Return', showing cancellation of 'how hast' and lay-out of first stanzas. (British Library MS Cotton Vespasian DVIII, f. 67).*

Chart of the lay-out of the earlier 'Life of Mary' play in the N-Town manuscript

f. no.	MS no.	Editorial title	Banns no.	Banns relationship
f. 37v	8	The Conception of Mary	—	not in Banns
f. 42	9	Mary in the Temple	—	not in Banns
f. 49	10	The Betrothal of Mary	8 and 9	two pageants in Banns; description occasionally close
f. 58v	11	The Parliament of Heaven and the Annunciation	10	no Parliament and description not close
f. 67	12	Joseph's Trouble about Mary	11	close but commonplace
f. 71	13	The Visitation	—	not in Banns

The scribe has numbered each pageant in the manuscript with a large red numeral; these are shown here in the 'MS no.' column. The titles given here are those used in the '*N-Town*' *Facsimile*. Each pageant of the earlier pageant series is numbered in the Banns; these are shown in the 'Banns no.' column, and in the final column is a brief indication of the similarity between the description of the pageant given in the Banns, and the pageant itself.

Pageants 8, 9 and 13 originally existed only as part of the 'Life of Mary' play; pageants 10 and 11 existed in separate versions in the 'Life of Mary' and the pageant series; and pageant 12 existed only in the pageant series.

and it is reasonable to assume that it is the one referred to in the Banns, and therefore from the earlier pageant series. On the surface it appears that this pageant, 'Joseph's Return', is simply presented as a separate pageant placed between two episodes of the 'Life of Mary' play. There are, however, one or two tell-tale signs of alteration which suggest that the main scribe made some attempt to blend it with the surrounding parts of the Mary play. First, at the end of the previous episode, 'The Parliament of Heaven and the Annunciation', there is a deleted stage direction: *And þan Mary seyth*. Secondly, in the middle of the first page of the Joseph pageant (see plate 3) are the words 'how hast', deleted; and thirdly, the opening of the following episode, 'The Visitation', seems like an abrupt breaking into the middle of a speech. None of these is in itself sufficient to suggest alteration of pageant and play to blend the two, but together they form a pattern. As there was no Joseph episode in the earlier Mary play, 'The Parliament of Heaven' should run straight on to 'The Visitation'; *and þan Mary seyth* should lead to a speech of Mary's. If one removes 'Joseph's Return', this is what happens, but it makes the transition very abrupt from the departure of Gabriel and no Joseph, in the 'Parliament', to Mary talking to Joseph in the 'Visitation' as though part of a continuing conversation.

What of the deleted 'how hast'? It occurs between Joseph's, 'I haue sore laboryd for þe and me', and Mary's, 'Husbond ryght gracyously now come be ȝe' ('N-Town', p. 109, lines 12 and 13). The same words, 'how hast', begin line 21, and it looks as though the scribe was originally going straight from line 12 to line 21. Is it possible that lines 13–20 are intruders here? And that they were originally part of the 'Visitation' or of a passage linking the 'Parliament' and the 'Visitation'? If we take out the possibly intrusive passage (ll. 13–20) from 'Joseph's Return' and link it with the surrounding episodes, the end of the 'Parliament' and the beginning of the 'Visitation', the section then reads:

Angeli cantando istam sequenciam ('with an angel singing this sequence'): *Aue Maria gratia plena dominus tecum uirgo serena* ('Hail Mary, full of grace, the Lord is with thee, fair virgin'). *And þan Mary seyth:*

Maria	Husbond, ryght gracyously now come be 3e.
	It solacyth me sore, sothly, to se 3ow in syth.
Joseph	Me merveylyth, wyff, surely, 3our face I cannot se,
	But as þe sonne with his bemys quan he is most bryth.
Maria	Husbond, it is as it plesyth oure Lord, þat grace of hym grew.
	Who þat evyr beholdyth me, veryly,
	They xal be grettly steryd to vertu;
	For þis 3yfte and many moo, good Lord, gramercy!
	Bvtt, husbond, of oo thynge I pray 3ow most mekely:
	I haue knowyng þat oure cosyn Elyzabeth with childe is,
	þat it plese 3ow to go to here hastyly,
	If owught we myth comforte here, it wore to me blys.

(my punctuation)

The appearance of Joseph is still a little sudden, but not impossibly so; the abruptness of the breaking into a conversation at the beginning of the 'Visitation' is removed; and interestingly the second stanza (previously lines 17–20 of 'Joseph's Return') fits with the rhyme scheme of the first quatrain from the 'Visitation'. Moreover, lines 13–20 fitted badly into 'Joseph's Return', being written in longer lines and with more elaborate language, but the passage now seems quite natural. It is finally worth noting that the reference to Mary's shining face leads more naturally to an accepting Joseph, as in the 'Visitation', than to the suspicious Joseph of 'Joseph's Return'. Curiously enough the scribe could have avoided the business of blending pageant and play altogether if he had followed the normal order of events and placed Joseph's return/trouble after and not before the Visitation, and thus after the end of the 'Life of Mary' play.

We are not in a position to say for certain that this *was* the form of the earlier Mary play (that is perhaps something that we shall never know) but at least it makes sense of the surviving evidence and puts us a stage nearer to a unique dramatic form. It also provides further evidence of the methods of the main scribe in his adaptation of his material.

Manuscripts are a fascinating study in themselves, and the manuscripts of the late medieval English mystery plays are no exception. It is, however for what they can tell us about the organisation, the staging and the nature of that drama, as well as for providing texts, that they demand investigation.

'Apparell comlye'

Meg Twycross

Trying to find out about fifteenth- and sixteenth-century English mystery-play costume from the available written evidence is a bit like trying to visualize the costumes of a National Theatre season from one published script and what remains of the annual audit after a freak wind has blown half the bills away over Waterloo Bridge for ever, and scattered the other half at random along the river-front. First you have to rearrange what you've got; then you have to comb it for references to costume, as opposed to actors' wages, stage carpentry, and the entertainment allowance (which, in medieval popular theatre, seems to bulk remarkably large). Even so, the type of information they give is bound to be elliptical, as they were writing for people who knew what they were talking about, so they had no need to describe in detail, and they were mainly interested in what the article or service cost, not what it looked like. Even the occasional inventory gives you just enough to identify each garment. Extend the problem by the fact that these accounts and records are spread over the best part of two hundred years, and that you will be lucky if you get a consecutive run for ten of them; that they come from different cities, towns, and villages, and there is no guarantee that costumes were the same in Coventry as they were in York; and that there is even no guarantee that the script which you have relates in any way to the accounts that have survived, as scripts were revised and re-written just as costumes were repaired and re-made: and you will see why chapters on staging in books on medieval theatre tend to be a brightly-coloured patchwork of bits and pieces, picked up from different towns and even from different countries, and placing an entry from 1433 cheek by jowl with one from 1573 as if they were contemporaries.

However, the situation is not quite as desperate as it might at first seem. We are dealing with a traditional form of theatre, where we may expect a certain continuity of staging and costume. Besides this, the *REED* scheme is currently systematically turning up new material and publishing it with more familiar records in a series of comprehensive collections. It seems a good time to pause and take stock. I want here to sketch in what you can, what you ought to be able to, and what you probably can't work out about the mystery play wardrobe from the currently available verbal evidence, confining myself strictly to material from Britain.

There is, however, one great difficulty about confining oneself to the verbal evidence: it is, strictly speaking, impossible. You have to visualize what the words are talking about: and the quality of your visualization will depend on your visual and, in the case of materials, on your tactile experience as well. There are several problems here, some obvious, some less so. We no longer have fabrics which we call *say* or *sendal*, or garments which we call a *kirtle* or a *coif*. Thus we have to go back and try to find out, from dictionaries, from pictures, from surviving garments and textiles, what precisely these were like: but at least we are aware that we don't know. On the other hand, we do have *coats*, *skirts*, and *jackets*; we still use *canvas* and *buckram*. But these are not necessarily the same garments or the same textiles as the ones which appear by those names in the fifteenth and sixteenth centuries. Then there are the half-concealed problems: we no longer wear *doublets* and *hose*, *cloaks* or *gowns* (except for the dressing- and academic varieties) but we think we know what they looked like, largely from Shakespeare plays and 'medieval' pictures. But two hundred years is a long time, and fashions change, and what Shakespeare meant by a *doublet* was not what John Paston, for example, meant by one, and the Coventry Cappers' Pilate had one made in 1549 which, if it were in contemporary fashion (of which we can't be sure), would be different yet again. Or familiar objects may be disguised under strange names: *spangles* are nothing more nor less than sequins; *tilsent blewe* is blue lamé.

Another problem is that they were writing about stage costume, not everyday clothes. I shall come back to this, as it is an important and still largely unexplored question, despite pioneer work by Hildburgh and Anderson, and recent fascinating work by Stella Mary Newton.[1] That there were certain stage conventions is clear from references to objects like *the farryshe* (Pharisee's) *hatt* (*REED Coventry*, p. 259) and *v prophets cappes* ('Chelmsford' p. 107). What exactly a Pharisee's hat or a prophet's cap looked like we can only speculate on from visual evidence, and again, there is the possibility that they were different in different periods. It is also highly probable that they used the words *gown*, *doublet*, *cote*, and so on as approximations, as we might say 'Pilate's suit' or 'the Virgin's headscarf'. The mere use of the words need not imply they were wearing everyday clothes.

Finally, there are some things which we might never guess without pictures to tell us: that angels wore feathered cat-suits, for example, or that Pilate was seen as a Turkish Pasha rather than a Roman governor.

Before we proceed to account books, we should look at the scripts themselves to see what information they can give us. It is however relatively rare for a playwright to specify what his characters are to wear. One exception is the morality play of *Wisdom who is Christ*. The stage directions give detailed costume instructions, and it would be tempting to take the description of Wisdom himself, the Second Person of the Trinity, as evidence of how God might be dressed in, say, the Creation play of a mystery cycle, especially as we have no record evidence except for the *face and heare* ('mask and wig') *for the Father* in the 1565 inventory of the Norwich Grocers' play of the Fall (*Non-Cycle Plays*, p. xxxv): all our evidence is for a Christ figure in leather or canvas body-suit and red cloak. But though the splendour is probably authentic – we have plenty of evidence from court masques and disguisings of masks *with Berdes of damaske gold*[2] – this God is more King (and Bridegroom) than Priest: we should substitute a cope for the mantle.

The costumes in *Wisdom* are meticulously described because it is a morality with masque-like qualities, where the costume is meant to speak emblematically. This is usually seen as a feature of morality rather than mystery plays, though Anima's transformation probably echoes the symbolic change of costume when Lucifer and his angels fall:

> We, that were angels so fare . . .
> Now are we waxen blak as any coyll,   *coal*
> and vgly, tatyrd as a foyll   *fool*
>   (*Towneley, Play 1*, lines 134, 136–7)

The garb of the Black and White Souls in the Doomsday plays equally makes their moral status clear, and it is possible that mystery play costume was more emblematic than we realize.

The only mystery play script that comes near to *Wisdom* in detailed attention to costume is the N-Town Passion Play, whose author is not only a very visual playwright, but also interested in the accuracy of his Biblical costume. Otherwise costume stage directions are sparse, presumably because the costume of Biblical characters was traditional, and could safely be left to the discretion of the producer. When they do appear, they draw attention either to some important effect which must not be overlooked: *Here xall Lazar aryse, trossyd wyth towellys, in a shete* (Digby, p. 54), or to changes of costume or disguise: *hic venit ihesus in apparatu peregrini* ('Here Jesus comes in the gear of a pilgrim', *Towneley*, p. 328). In *The Conversion of St Paul*, the playwright specifies that Saul must first appear *goodly besene in þe best wyse, lyke an aunterous* (errant) *knyth* (*Digby*, p. 1), but after his conversion *Her apperyth Saule in a disciplis wede* (*Digby*, p. 15), which is interesting not only in that the change of clothes symbolizes a change of heart, but also because it shows there was a conventional *disciplis wede*. Others stipulate on-stage changes: the author of the N-Town Passion Play is responsible for one of the longest of these, because he allows far more of the action to take place without words:

> and qwan *he is skorgyd · þei put upon hym A cloth of sylk and settyn*   *when*
> *hym on a stol and puttyn A kroune of þornys on hese hed with forkys*
> *and þe jewys knelying to cryst* takyng *hym A septer and skornyng*   *giving*
> *hym. and þan þei xal pullyn of þe purpyl cloth and don on A-geyn his*
> *owyn clothis . . .*   ('N-Town', p. 294)

In other versions of this scene we have to work out what is happening from the dialogue. The Chester Christ wears a surprising number of layers of clothing: at the Crucifixion each of the four soldiers gets a garment before they sit down to dice for the seamless robe.

Any mystery play designer is strongly counselled to read the dialogue itself in some detail, as the characters tend to comment on each others' clothes. In the Chester Cycle Joseph refuses to approach the Doctors in the Temple because their *furres fine* intimidate him; the Mothers of the Innocents threaten to beat the Knights over their *bassnetts* (helmets) . . . *bygge & broade*; Antichrist sneers at Enoch and Elijah as thieves because they are *muffeled in mantelles*. Rarely, the script gives a complete costume description, like that of the Chester Serpent:

> A maner of an edder is in this place   *adder*
> that wynges like a bryde shee hase –   *bird*
> feet as an edder, a maydens face –
> hir kynde I will take . . .   *nature*
> the edders coate I will take one   *on*
>   (*Chester Play II*, lines 193–6, 206)

This at least gives some idea of how Satan is to change into the Serpent, a problem which other playwrights sidestep, leaving the director to worry over the practicalities of 'In a worme liknes wil!e Y wende' (*York*, p. 65, line 23). However, sometimes the text can be puzzling or even misleading until the records give us supplementary evidence. The Serpent of the Norwich Grocers' Fall *Play B* says 'angell of lyght I shew mysylfe to be' (line 40). There was an apocryphal tradition that 'the devil when tempting took the form not of a serpent, but of an angel of light'[3], and the dialogue suggests a quite different costume: but the Norwich Grocers' 1565 inventory lists *A cote with hosen and tayle for the Serpente, steyned* ('painted, dyed') *with a with* ('white') *heare (Non-Cycle Plays*, p. xxxv), which shows that it was like an angel only in its upper half. In 1534, the wig was called *a new heer, with a crown for the Serpent*, and in 1556 they also hired *a hear and crowne for the Angell*, so the angel-likeness would have been marked.[4]

We also have the official Banns from Chester, early (1539–40) and late (a post-Reformation set recorded in 1608–9, long after the plays' demise); and the official list, dating from 1415 but with additions and alterations, of the York mystery plays, recorded in the city's Memorandum Book. Each gives us scraps of information about costume. The Chester Banns tells the Butchers to

> Set out as accustomablie vsed haue ye
> The Deuell in his ffeathers. all Rugged and rente
> (*REED Chester*, p. 244)

and contains the famous post-Reformation struggle of sensibility over the problem of presenting God on stage, with a gold face. The York list really only confirms the expected: *Iuuenis sedens ad sepulcrum indutus albo* ('A young man seated at the sepulchre dressed in white'); *Iesus lucas & Cleophas in forma peregrinorum* ('Jesus, Lucas and Cleophas in the garb of pilgrims').

The bulk of our supplementary evidence comes from guild accounts and other official papers. Here the information is often frustratingly of the type you would expect from an account book:

> Item payd for þe demons garment makyng & þ[e] stof vs iiijd ob.
> (Coventry Smiths, 1451)

> Inprimis to Jhesus for gloves & all xxij d
> (Coventry Smiths, 1477)

> Item for dimidium (half) ȝard of cloth to god iij d
> (York Mercers, 1461)

Nonetheless, one should be able to deduce certain things even from the amounts spent on materials and making. How did they compare in price with real clothes, for example? Did the plays make do with cheaper materials? Which costume was the most lavish? Were any radical changes made in the costuming of the same character over the years? Did the sums spent on costume vary from town to town, from guild to guild? No one has yet, as far as I know, attempted to analyse this systematically, though R. W. Ingram has done some very interesting work on Coventry,[5] and it would be a complicated exercise in economic history, involving price fluctuations from season to season and from city to city.

The main problem is that we really have very little data that can profitably be compared, even from the major cities. Surviving accounts have great chronological gaps in them. Most of the York information ends before the Chester even begins. (One thing that surprises newcomers to the field is that the bulk of our record information on the 'medieval' mystery plays comes from the mid and even late sixteenth century.) Then, whether by accident of survival or because they had different accounting habits, the three major sets of records, York, Chester, and Coventry, provide very different sorts of information. Coventry has quite a lot on costume but not much on overall organization: York has a great deal on organization but hardly anything on costume. They also vary from guild to

34

guild and from period to period. Some companies itemize expenses in detail: some, like the Coventry Weavers until 1541, may merely present an overall total: *Item, spend on corpus crysty day xxvj s iiij d* (1528).

One can try one or two experiments, but they need a solid background of comparative material. For example, garments for 'God' (Christ) seem to stay remarkably within the same price range, between guild and guild, period and period, and city and city. In 1554 the Coventry Smiths paid 3s *for v schepskens for gods coot & for makyng*; three years later the Drapers also gave their Christ a new costume, and paid 3s for seven skins and *the baryll for the yerthe quake*. In 1563 they again paid 3s *for A Cooate for god and for A peyre of gloues ffor hym*, the pair of gloves, which around then cost 2d, being apparently equivalent to the price of the barrel. A century earlier, in 1452, the Smiths had paid 22% less, 2s 4d overall, for *vj skynnys of whitleder to godds garment* and *for makyng of the same garment*; ten years later and in another city, the York Mercers also paid 2s 4d *for the cloth of god sarke & þe hose makyng & payntyng*. But it is difficult to say what conclusions we can draw from this.

The amounts spent on mystery play costumes come nowhere near the amounts spent on costumes for the Court revels, where satin and cloth of gold are the order of the day, but compare well with the grants made by the cities for official liveries. In 1452 the Coventry Smiths paid 24s 10½d *for makyng of iiij gownnys and iiij hodds to þe tormentors and þe stof þat went þerto*; in 1442 the City Waits received 20s between four for their liveries. The most expensive garments on record belong to the Coventry Herod: 13s 8d for a gown in 1489, made up of 7s 4d for the garment itself and another 6s 4d *for peynntyng and stenyng theroff*. In 1502 this painted gown was replaced by one of satin and blue buckram costing 21s for materials and making: the Common Clerk of York was at the same time receiving 20s a year for his livery.[6]

We can glean a fair amount about the range of materials used in making costumes, though our information is biased in that we mainly have repair and replacement entries for the costumes which were under the greatest strain, either because the characters were physically active or even violent, like Herod and Pilate, or because the garments were close-fitting, like those of the devils, the saved and damned souls, and Christ, and materials were not so elastic then – knitted fabrics only really appear in the second half of the sixteenth century (apart from caps), and then only as hose. We thus get a preponderance of the tough materials: leather, buckram, and canvas.

If we are to visualize what the costumes themselves looked and felt like to wear, we have to know something about the nature of these materials at the time. Leather, which for us is a luxury commodity, was fairly cheap. Most frequently, it is used for what seem to have been close-fitting bodysuits. *Gods kote of leddur* turns up not only in Coventry, but in Chelmsford, New Romney in Kent, and Tewkesbury.[7] *Whitleder*, which was used not only for *godds garment* but also for the suits of Adam and Eve in the Cornish *Creacion of the World*,[8] was not white as such, but selfcoloured, being leather that has been tawed (not tanned) and left undyed. It would thus be as near to skin in colour and texture as a simulation could get, and could be tailored close to the contours of the body in a way stiffer materials of a similar weight could not. Gilded leather was also used for trimming and 'guarding' other garments.

Canvas seems to have been used as an alternative to leather. From 1538–55, the White Souls of the Coventry Drapers' Doomsday play had cotes apparently made of leather, whereas the Black Souls had *shyrts & hose* made of canvas: then in 1557 when the costumes were refurbished for a new version of the play, both white and black souls were dressed in canvas, dyed black for the Black Souls but, surprisingly, yellow for the White Souls. Canvas seems to have been preferred for the devil's costume, presumably because it was easier to sew hair onto it (1568, 1572). It could also be painted, by far the most usual form of decoration, on which large sums of money were expended, sometimes far in excess of the cost of the original material:

```
Item ffor makyng of iiij Jaketes          ij s
Item ffor iiij ellne clothe ffor the jakkets & the hatts   xviij d
Item p[ai]d to the pynnter ffor hys warkemonchipe        xxj s vii d
                                        (Coventry Smiths, 1502)
```

Canvas was used for a wide range of garments and stage properties, from the camels of the Three Wise Men (*Malone VII* p. 189: Canterbury 1501) to *pylates doblet* (Coventry Cappers, 1549). It was presumably fairly heavy and resilient, able to take a fair amount of strain without ripping: but the word seems to cover a much wider range of fabric weight and weave than it does nowadays, and we find it used where we might use calico or drill (cotton being a new and expensive yarn), to make sheets and even shirts, though most usually for linings. The fact that Pilate's doublet was of canvas does not necessarily mean that it was a rough stage garment: canvas doublets, trimmed with lace and puffed with taffeta, were fashionable (see Linthicum, pp. 96–7), and the Revels inventory for 1562 includes canvas with silver stripes (Feuillerat *Elizabeth*, p. 114, p. 136).

Buckram was nothing like the glue-stiffened material we know today. Originally it was a fine cotton material, used for vestments and linings: later, by the fifteenth century, it seems to have been heavier and used for hangings as well as linings. The Coventry Drapers' Souls proceeded from leather to canvas to buckram, back to canvas, and back to buckram again (1543–71), which suggests that the weight and texture were similar. Blue buckram was used to line Herod's gown, and the 1490 Smiths' wardrobe also had *iiij Jakketts of blake bokeram for þe tormentors with nayles & dysse upon þem* and two others of buckram *with hamers crowned,* which suggests that it too could be painted. The Revels wardrobe used it for linings and making *patrons,* presumably toiles that could be sewn up cheaply (Feuillerat *Elizabeth* p. 83: 1558).

Of the finer materials we only get glimpses. *Saye,* which was 'a soft, light, finely twilled fabric made in both silk and wool' (Linthicum, p. 87) was used for *Gods apparell* in the Coventry Cappers' inventory of 1567. It has also given rise to the most famous ghost property in theatrical history, the *halfe a yard of rede sea* (Sharp, p. 64: undated),[9] which sounds romantic but probably merely provided the facing for a gown or a rather large patch. The Drapers clothed their Christ in *Redde Sendall* (1565) 'a thynne stuffe lyke sarcenette' (fine soft lining silk) 'and of a rawe kynde of sylke or sarcenett, but courser, and narrower, then the Sarcenett nowe ys' (*OED* sb. *sendal,* quoting Thynne in 1599: he implies that as a fabric it has gone out of fashion). The Coventry Smiths' Tormentors had, beside their buckram jackets, four *of an other suett wythe damaske fflowers* (1490), which sounds indecorously colourful until we compare them with a set from Bodmin in Cornwall which were *of satyn of bryddes* (birds) *of yelo and blue* (Bakere, p. 22).

After the Reformation (though often not till the 1560s) amateur dramatic societies descended upon the sales of Popish vestments and bore them off, either to use as they stood – the *bysschops taberd of scarlet that we bought in the trenete church* for 10s in 1544 may have been worn by the Coventry Smiths' Annas or Caiaphas, though we cannot prove it – or to be cut up *to make players garments* (Chester Trinity Churchwardens, 1569/70). Many of the smaller towns and villages profited from this sudden windfall: in Chelmsford the wardrobe belonging to the church included garments made of red velvet, blue velvet, red satin, cloth of tissue (woven with silver or gold and silk), and red *bawdekyn* (a form of brocade with raised figures in colour on cloth of gold) ('Chelmsford', p. 107). The Bodmin Tormentors had an alternative set of *cotes made of a sewt of vestyments for goode frydayes* (Bakere, p. 22).

However, even before church vestments came on the market, players' garments were being made out of cast-off clothing in a very familiar fashion. John Rastell's wardrobe was for interludes rather than mysteries, but it provides useful comparative evidence.[10] A peculiarly complete description of it survives from around 1530, because it was the subject of a lawsuit, and several witnesses, including the tailor who had made them, were called in to swear to the garments in detail, with material, colour, yardage, and estimated value. Though the materials were sumptuous: satin, sarcenet and saye, besides the buckram linings and the trimming of gold kid and white cat's fur, they were in fact made out of cast-offs 'And if they had been bought of new stuff it would have cost much more money' – almost twice as much, claimed Rastell – and they were pieced and *paned* (striped in different colours) in a way that was not only currently fashionable, but would also have enabled the tailor to select the best pieces. One garment, for example, was 'paned with yellow, green, red, and blue sarcenet, and lined with old red buckram', and there was 'A woman's garment, of green and blue sarcenet, checked and lined with red buckram', worth 24s, that the tailor thought was 'made in quarrels ('diamonds') or lozenges, he remembreth not whether, and was a busy work, and Mistress Rastell did help to sew that, and part of the gallant's gown also'.

Each of the garments seems to have contained about seven or eight yards of material, save two, which contained twelve yards, one a 'garment for a priest to play in, of red say'. Priests' garments appear to have been cut circular, and thus use a considerable yardage;[11] but the difficulty in trying to work out whether a particular garment was flowing or skimpy from the amount of material bought to make it is that fabrics were made in widely differing widths: most linens and woollens were probably 45″ wide (the clothiers' ell), though broadcloth could be 72″, but the finer and more expensive silks were woven on narrow looms and were usually 27″ wide or even narrower.[12] Thus in the Court Revels accounts, where cloth of gold, silks, and brocades were ordered by the yard from the Wardrobe or straight from the mercer, enormous yardages seem to be used. In the pageant of *the Golldyn Arber in the Arche yerd* ('orchard') *of Plesyer* presented in Whitehall in 1511, the King and his five companions used 39 yards of shining blue satin, 21¾ yards of blue velvet for Milan bonnets, and 8½ yards of cloth of gold for hose: William Cornish wore a gown of 14 yards (only slightly more ample than the priest's garment belonging to Rastell), and six ladies wore gowns of 14 yards of green and white satin, seven yards of each. (Brewer and Gairdner, II pt. 2, 1495–6). All this contrasts sharply with the 2½ yards *of flaxson clauth to make meyre madelentes coute* bought by the Chester Cordwainers in 1549/0, but it is probable that the linen was twice or even three times the width of the satin, and that the *cote* was a closefitting garment rather than a gown with flowing skirts and wide sleeves.

To be able to work out square yardages might provide one more clue in solving such problems as, for example, what precisely the accounts mean when they talk of a *cote*, especially when used of the costume of God, the Devil, the Serpent, Adam and Eve, and the Souls. This apparently all-purpose word points up the kind of problems we have over terminology. As part of ordinary attire, the *coat* clearly changed its shape many times over two hundred years, but the word seems to have been used of a garment performing a certain kind of function, or perhaps one should say, with a certain type of status in the hierarchy of garments. It was clearly less ample than the *gown* – 3½ yards go to make a livery gown in Chester in 1588, and only 1½ to a coat – and worn underneath it – the Wakefield Noah says 'Now my gowne will I cast and wyrk in my cote' (*Towneley Play* 3, line 262). It was worn over the shirt, which was worn next to the skin, as witness the proverb 'Nere is my cote but nerer is my shyrt' (*OED* sb. *coat*, 1539). In the fourteenth and early fifteenth centuries it was usually used of the *cote hardi*, a formfitting garment worn by both sexes, but also of the heraldic garment worn over armour, for example. All this suggests that if we abstract its essence, as opposed to the accidents of fashion, it was the lowest layer of garment that could be worn on top with decency, as opposed to appearing in your shirt and drawers: made of 'top-layer' material, but revealing the figure: if one can rob them of their social status and informal connotations, the equivalent of T-shirt and jeans as opposed to either business suit or vest and underpants. If this were so, it would be the nearest approximate term for a body-stocking, but still available for the garments of tormentors and banner bearers.

This still does not tell us exactly how form-fitting it was, or even what shape it was. It seems to have been made out of relatively small yardages, and to have gone with hose, to which it was laced in the normal fashion with points: the Coventry Drapers, who regularly buy six dozen points at a time, specify in 1566 that they are *for ye souls & the demons*. This suggests some kind of close-fitting suit joined at waist or hips. With Adam and Eve, the Souls, and 'God' (the naked Christ-figure of the Passion, Resurrection, and Doomsday) it clearly represented nudity: God's leather garment even had hands to match (Coventry Smiths 1499), and over it the Coventry Drapers' Doomsday God wore what sounds like the traditional red cloak: in 1565 they bought *iij yards of Redde Sendall* for him.

In York, however, the garment worn by the Doomsday Christ and Souls is called a *sark*, not a *cote*. *Sark* normally means 'shirt', and Christ's *Sirke Wounded* (Mercers 1433) suggests to the modern reader a nightshirt with a heraldic device painted on the front. This may show us that mystery play costume conventions were not the same across the country: on the other hand, in Coventry (1538) two adjacent entries for the Doomsday plays give the *blakke Soules shyrts & hose* and then refer *to Coloryng & makyng the same cots*, so *sirke* may be an approximation in the same way as *cote*.

We can deduce quite a lot from the accounts about the organization of the wardrobe side of the production. Mystery play cycles, which were repeated year after year, did not design an entirely new wardrobe for each performance. Instead, as one might expect, the same costumes are used over and over again, with occasional entries for repairs and sometimes for the replacement of a garment. Since the Coventry guilds, for example, seem to try to keep their expenditure fairly level from year to year, this would again

39

presumably be a matter of good housekeeping: once pressing repairs had been dealt with, if there was still some pageant money in the kitty one year, they could afford to make Herod a new doublet. Occasionally they seem to have decided on a total overhaul: *these bene the Garments that wer newe reparellyd a gaynst corpus christi day . . .* (Coventry Smiths, 1490). But even when one guild took over the responsibility and *pleyng geire* for a play from another guild (*REED Coventry*, p. 131), they do not seem to have redesigned the set and costumes. In 1557 the Coventry Drapers seem to have radically overhauled and (possibly) redesigned their wardrobe to go with a new script, but this is about the only evidence we have of this sort of proceeding. Someone must at the beginning have designed and paid for a whole new set of costumes, unless each actor was made personally responsible for his own – though the fact that the wardrobe then became the responsibility of the guild argues against this. At Lincoln in 1515 we have some evidence of pressure being brought to bear on the important men of the town to costume a procession in much this way, but as an answer to the problem that because of plague in the city *ye knyghtes & gentylmen* in the country are afraid to loan garments for the St. Anne's Day pageants: *wherfore euery Alderman Schall prepare & Setfoorth in ye Seid Arrey ij good gownes And euery Scheryff pere Agowne And euery Chaumberlen pere Agowne & the persons w^t Theym to weyre ye same* (*Malone VIII*, p. 43). Later it is decreed that the Aldermen are to provide silk gowns for the Kings, and the Sheriffs cloth gowns for the prophets, a nice social distinction: but these are only loans made for the occasion, and do not become part of a permanent wardrobe (*Malone VIII*, pp. 51, 52).

We must thus wonder if the costumes were designed at all, in our sense. It is almost impossible to tell. There is certainly no evidence that an artist was engaged to do so for a whole cycle, as he was for similar religious pageants in the Netherlands. However, when in 1541 Henry VIII announced his intention of coming to York, the Mayor *callid certen Ioyners and paynters of this City and commaundyd them Immedyatly to taike yer Consaille and deuyses togydders to maike a showe at Mikkellythbarre*, and it seems likely that costume designing followed the same pattern: some craftsman with a flair would be told off to make a costume for Herod, and would in effect design it. The painters, who were engaged to decorate everything from Herod's gown to the demon's head, were probably most responsible for the look of the production: it would probably have a random design but highly professional finish – except that folk-art tends to impose a highly elaborated style of its own which overrides individual tastes.

By the time we catch up with them, in the major cities each guild has a stock wardrobe which is the official legal responsibility of the pageant master or masters. Each item was checked at hand-over against an official inventory, several of which survive, from York (Mercers and Creed Play), Coventry (Cappers), Norwich (Grocers), and Beverley (Hairsters). In the smaller towns and villages they were usually the responsibility of the churchwardens, who also kept inventories.

These inventories show that the wardrobe by no means provided the entire costume for every character, even when we are sure that the entire cast list was. The York Mercers 1433 wardrobe list, for example, contains

iiij Aubes (albs) for iiij Appostels
iij diademes with iij vesernes (masks) for iij Appostels
iiij diademes with iiij Cheuelers (wigs) of ʒalow for iiij Apostels.

If they depended solely on this wardrobe for their costumes, they could have fitted out four Apostles with albs, yellow wigs, and haloes from stock, which leaves three haloes with masks for three naked Apostles, and nothing at all for the remaining five – if the play actually featured all twelve Apostles, as the 1415 Banns suggests. So either there were only four Apostles, and rather more costumes than necessary, perhaps because a set had been broken and had to be replaced, or because the costumes had got out of date (the Coventry Smiths in 1490 had two complete matching sets and a half set for the Tormentors): or they made up the rest of the wardrobe by borrowing albs from a cooperative chaplain who charged nothing and so did not get into the accounts. The rest of the cast are fairly adequately covered except for the angels, who have wings but again no albs. Sometimes items which we know existed do not appear in the inventory: the Coventry Cappers' Pilate had a gown, which was mended with green silk in 1576, and a cloak, mended in 1573, but only his doublet and his *hede* appear in the inventories of 1567 and 1591.

A number of these gaps were filled by hiring costumes. Some, as might be expected, are ecclesiastical: *to the clarke for lone of a Cope an Altercloth & Tunecle x d* (Chester Smiths for the Purification play, 1571). After the post-Reformation sales, private individuals hired out some of the stuff they had acquired: in 1570, the Chester Coopers hired two copes, presumably for Annas and Caiaphas, from William Rogerson. Certain people became specialist hirers: Harry Bennett of Coventry, a Capper, seems to have specialized in hair, and is not only paid by his own craft *for mendynge the demonn cote and makyng the head* in 1562, but also hires beards to the Weavers for a penny each (1570–72). Other individuals seem to have one garment they are known to be willing to hire: the Coventry Smiths hired *Mr. Wygson's gowne* for Herod from at least 1567 to 1574. Women's gowns are frequently hired.

The guilds themselves hired out costumes from their wardrobes: in 1561 the York Goldsmiths, clearly worried in case their Magi costumes were being lent round free to oblige friends and acquaintances, laid down

that neither the Corones nor gownes be lent to any
vnder viij d a pece / And that it be paid or they be delyvered   *before*
Except it be to some of thoccupacion and the Serchars to   *craft*
make Accompte therof.

A century earlier, somebody with a stock of angels' wings was hiring them
to the York Mercers. Possibly this was a guild which had performed earlier
in the day, perhaps the Barkers who played the Creation, and would have
had time to disrobe and hand the wings over for a second airing at the Day
of Judgement?

Other gaps must have been filled in ways so obvious as to go unnoticed.
People who had always played a certain part might have slipped into the
habit of keeping the costume at home. The Bodmin tormentors' costumes
were at the time of the inventory *inkepyng one with John Vyvyan, a noder
with Thomas Bligh, the 3rd with Nicholas Opy, and the 4th with Richard
Corant* (Bakere, p. 22). Others may have lent them free, as opposed to
'lending' them against a quart of wine and so escaped getting into the
accounts. In 1521 the Lincoln authorities, again short of costumes because
of the plague, determine that *Mr Alanson Schalbe Instantly desyryd To
bowro Agowne of my lady powes for one of the Maryes* (*Malone VIII*,
p. 49), and the small groups in Suffolk seem to have been in the habit of
begging local notables for the loan of garments. Most guilds possessed or
hired armour for the annual Watch, and dressed their Knights in that.

Getting ready for the play developed into a fullscale party: *Item for potes
of ale when we dressed oure playes & when we made oure capes & cotes vj d*
record the Chester Painters and Glaziers in 1568. *Bowning* ('getting
ready') sometimes involved make-up and the fastening on of false beards,
as nowadays: but actually getting into the garments and securing them was
a more laborious business than in these days of zipfasteners and press-
studs. Besides the ubiquitous knotting of points, the actors seem to have
been pinned into their costumes in what sounds like a perilous fashion but
was in fact quite normal in everyday life:

> payed for pines to drese the woma[n]s clothes abowte heare and to piyne the
> dye menes ('demons') covtes jd
>
> (Chester Innkeepers, 1596/7)

and even sewn into them:

> payed for thryd and pynes one mydsomeɩ even to sowe the chylldes clothes
> vpone hime jd
>
> (Chester Joiners, 1583/4)

One understands why *bowning* and, afterwards, *unbowning*, was such a
thirsty business.

On the day of the performance, special arrangements seem to have been
made for actors who doubled two parts. Someone seems to have been

taken on to carry the other set of clothes and, presumably, assist in the change. The usual interpretation of the two entries in 1572 and 1574 of the Chester Coopers' accounts:

> payde for the carynge of pylates clothes vi d

and

> paied vnto pylat and to him that carried arrates clothes . . .

is that Pilate and Herod were doubled.

Between performances, routine maintenance was carried out. The costumes were brushed to clean them (*Malone IX*, p. 8: Sherborne 1551, 1553), though only the linen garments could be washed: the Coventry Cappers frequently pay *for wasscheng ye angelles albes*. Any embroidery had to be taken off and then replaced after washing: at Canterbury, where a play of the Martyrdom of St. Thomas with real blood meant that the costumes *had* to be washed after each performance, expenses include *for wasshyng of the albe the auterclothes & settyng onne a gayn of the apparell* (*Malone VII*, p. 197: 1531). Usually, however, garments were brightened by sending them to the painter, and properties smartened with new *colours and gold foyle & sylver foyle* (Coventry Smiths, 1500).

What general conclusions can we draw about the appearance of the costumes? I must emphasize that whatever they are, they are bound to be partial. York had 51 mystery plays in its heyday: we have one set of records, the Mercers', which give us any detail about costumes, plus two which are minimal. Chester is slightly better: of 23 plays (25 at the most), we have six sets of accounts: but two of these do not even begin until after the plays are over for good, and are only of interest because characters from the plays are preserved in the Midsummer Show. Coventry is by far the best: for ten plays four sets of accounts, though only one, the Smiths', goes back as far as the fifteenth century. On the other hand, only two Coventry plays survive, and only one, the Weavers', corresponds with a set of accounts.

The wardrobe must have been traditional. It was not like a modern production, or even like the Court masques and disguisings, where a new set of costumes was designed for each event. From 1541, when the Coventry Weavers started itemizing their pageant expenses, to 1579, the last year the cycle was played, the guild spends almost nothing on costume. They make a mitre once (1542), hire an amice twice (1541, 1543); in 1564, in a sudden rush of extravagance, they alter one of Jesus' sleeves, paint his 'head' (?wig ?mask), and sole his hose. In 1570 they start hiring beards from Harry Bennett, and in 1576 add a cape or cap; in 1577 they mend the two angels' crowns. The only regular payment for clothes is for gloves for the cast, which seems to be an annual honorarium. Either the play (the

Purification) was so staid that the wardrobe remained in good repair and therefore identical, for forty years, or the characters were meant to pay for minor repairs and changes out of their fees, which were slightly higher than those of the Cappers. In Continental religious processions, this longevity can make the costumes virtually iconic: but this may have happened with tableaux rather than plays.

On the other hand, the Smiths, Drapers and Cappers, partly again because of the nature of their plays, make a considerable number of alterations and renewals over the period of their accounts: not necessarily all at once, but updating garments gradually, year by year: Pilate's doublet one year, Annas and Caiaphas' gowns the next. We should remember that one can have new costumes without buying new material: even the extravagant Court Revels made over and cut down costumes until the long hanging sleeves of the Venetian Senators were *translated into hed peces & vndersleves for Turkes and ageyne from thence in to Shoes and nowe not Serviceable nor chargeable* (Feuillerat *Elizabeth*, p. 19). A fullscale revision, like that of the Drapers' new play in 1557 or the Smiths' general overhaul in 1490 would alter the look more obviously.

It is fairly often said, as in a recent and very useful survey of the medieval theatre, that 'contemporary clothing was usually worn by the majority of characters' (Tydeman, p. 209). This is unintentionally misleading, for it implies that the mystery plays were done in 'modern dress'. This rests on a couple of questionable assumptions: first that when the characters wear garments called *gowns* or *doublets*, these must be ordinary clothes: and second that Biblical characters in medieval pictures are wearing contemporary dress. For most people, as we can see only too clearly in mystery play revivals, the Middle Ages are a never-never period inhabited by colourful characters sporting styles ranging from the eleventh to the sixteenth century. In fact, not only can everyday fashions be dated fairly precisely, but you have only to compare the saints in a painting or a stained-glass window with the donors who often occupy the same picture-space to see that while the overall silhouette may be the same, they are wearing two quite different styles of garment. A little further study shows that Biblical costume can probably be divided into several distinct sub-categories, among which are disciples' garments, prophets' garments, Holy Women plain and gay (as they used to say of Quakers), *Sarrazins* of various classes, and Jewish ecclesiastics. Besides those who would have followed these conventions almost unconsciously, there were those who, like the author of the N-Town Passion, were interested in them in an antiquarian way. When he gives instructions that his Annas is to be dressed *after a busshop of þe hoold lawe*, he means precisely that: a Jewish High Priest, after the specifications in Exodus 28. The blue tabard is a version of the ephod, and the mitre, as he says, is not a modern one, but the High

44

Priest's tiara. I illustrate one fifteenth century scholarly reconstruction of this costume: there were others. There is no space here to go further into this fascinating topic: but we should realize that because Annas and Caiaphas are called 'bishops', that does not imply they are contemporary English bishops.

It also points up the way in which headgear can alter the whole feeling of a costume, something which modern mime-artists know. It is interesting that when the Coventry Smiths overhauled their wardrobe in 1490, almost half the list consisted of headgear: *a Creste for heroude . . . a hatt for pilatte*

Figure 1: *The High Priest's regalia from* Biblia cum postillis de Nicolas de Lyra *(Koberger, Nuremberg 1482) sig P6ʳ (BL 1B 7323).*

45

. . . a hatt for pilatts sone . . . ij myters for the bysschoppis . . . ij hatts for ij princes . . . iiij hatts for the tormentors . . . other ij hatts for the tormentors . . . ij Cheverels gyld for Jh[e]s[us] & petur . . . the devyls hede. These must surely be stage hats, even *Sarazyn* hats. Their view of what Biblical characters wore was conditioned by their knowledge of the Middle East, just as our conventional Nativity Play costume is conditioned by the engravings of the Bedouin brought back by nineteenth century travellers in

Figure 2: *'Sarrazins' (Arabs) fròm Breydenbach* Peregrinationes ad terram sanctam, *a popular travel book and guide to the Holy Land. From the Latin Version, 1486 (BL C 20e 3).*

Palestine. Their Middle East was *Sarrazin*, and turbanned: I illustrate a picture from the *Peregrinatio* of von Breydenbach, a very popular pilgrims' travel book published in 1486, for comparison with the Pilates and Herods of Biblical art.

The assumption that the characters are wearing 'contemporary' dress also rests on the fact that people are known to have left their own garments to the guilds for use in the pageants:

> Also I bequeth to the paionde of the same Crafte I am of my self my lyned scarlet gowne without ffurre and my Scarlet Cloke to be kept to serve theym in their said paionde the tyme of the playes And I bequeth to the Crafte of Tanners my lyned Crymsyn gowne not furred to the same vse
>
> (Will of William Pisford 1518, *REED Coventry*, p. 113)

and that garments, especially women's garments, were borrowed for use in the plays. But precisely when, and in what context, does an ordinary garment become a stage garment? when do a pair of bedroom slippers become Tudor shoes, or an Indian scarf a turban for a Wise Man? an evening dress a princess's robe? a vicar's cloak one for a villain? It is difficult for us, whose fashion is to dress down rather than to dress up, to reconstruct precisely how people would have seen certain types of flowing garments when they were worn sashed in a different way, with different headgear. There seems no reason why William Pisford's scarlet gown should not have graced as exotic a prophet as ever wore turban.

Nothing in the records suggests to me that the mystery play wardrobes were attempting to reproduce the contemporary scene. I have written elsewhere about the use of masks, the gilding of Christ's face even when he appears as Man on earth, and the stylized (and very covered-up) representation of nakedness on stage.[13] There are hints of an emblematic style of costuming in the 1490 Coventry Smiths' Tormentors, with their *Jakketts of blake bokeram . . . with nayles & dysse upon þem* and their other jackets *of bokeram with hamers crowned*, and in the stage direction to *Mary Magdalen: Here xall entyr þe thre Mariis arayyd as chast women* (as nuns?) *wyth sygnis of þe passyon pryntyd ypon þer brest* (*Digby*, p. 57). There is a naturalistic excuse for the Tormentors' Instruments of the Passion: they can be presented as coats of arms – but none at all for the Maries. The disciples of the York Last Supper appear, like the Apostles in the Creed Play, to have worn haloes (Bakers, 1553, 1557, 1569; Creed Play, 1465). Even the *disciplis wede*, the simple robe and mantle we see in art, would be interpreted emblematically:

> Comounly alle þe apostelys been peyntyd barefoot in tokene of innocence and of penaunce . . . Also þe apostolys comounly and othere seyntys been peyntyd wyt menttelys in tokene of þe vertue of pouert qheche þey haddyn. For, as seyȝt ('says') Seynt Gregory, alle þese wordly goodys been nought ellys but a clothyng to þe body, and a mentyl is a loos clothyng nought fest to þe body but loos and lyghtly may been doon awey ('easily taken off') and sone cast awey. Ryght soo, þe godys of þis word weryn but as a mentyl to þe apostolys and othere seyntys, for þey weryn alwey soo loos from here herte þat þey ȝeuyn noo gret tale þerof ('they did not set much store by them') ne to lesyn ('lose') hem . . . but alwey þey weryn redy to forsakyn al for Cristys sake.[14]

Often this stylization and use of emblem in the costumes comes as a shock to the reader of the plays, because it is coupled with, in the words, a tender naturalism of emotion which we feel should be expressed in a naturalism of staging. But the Christ calling on the audience to

> Byholdes myn heede, myn handis, and my feete
>
> (*York*, p. 321, line 255)

may well have been displaying these wounds painted on a canvas body-stocking: the Mary of the Chester Purification and Doctors play, maternally worried over losing her child in a strange town, was wearing a crown (1560–61). More than that, she was played by a man. The *pylatts wyfe* to whom *Maisturres grymesby* of Coventry lent her gear in 1488 was a man. The Norwich Eve, dressed in *cote* and *hosen*, whom the Serpent addressed as 'gemme of felicyté and femynyne love' was called Francis Fygot (*Non-Cycle Plays*, p. xxxii). Borrowing a gown *of my lady powes for one of the Maryes* (*Malone VIII*, p. 49) sounds like naturalism if we think of Mary Cleophas as a woman: if we think of him as a man it moves into a quite different range of artifice.

We have not enough information to know whether the English plays inclined towards the simple and relatively cheap in their costuming of sacred characters, or whether they followed the pattern of the play at Bourges in 1536, where St. Peter was 'dressed in a gown of crimson satin figured with gold, embellished with diamonds and large pearls, and a mantle hung crosswise of cloth of gold in raised patterns',[14] and the English Court interlude of 1527 where *Petar, Poull, and Jamys* were clad in *iij. abetts of whyghte sarsenet, and iij. red mantylls and heris of sylvar of damaske and pelleuns* ('palliums', archbishop's regalia) *of skarlet* (Brewer and Gairdner, IV, pt. 2, p. 1605). An inventory of vestments and regalia from Eton College in 1531[11] lists *a coote for our lady of (tynsyl cloth of gold orfrayd with ryd cloth of tyssewe) with saynt Jamys shell pomegarnare & the gryfyn yn the hemne of hit*, and probably this richness was the ideal to which the mystery plays would have aspired rather than that of tasteful simplicity. It not only had an emblematic function, betokening *þe blisse þat þey been now inne, nought þe aray þat þey haddyn vpon erthe*, but also showed the honour in which they were held.[17] By costuming their characters lavishly, the guilds would show how highly they held the real saints whom they represented, and the God in whose honour the plays were performed. It would also, of course, make a major contribution to the guild's prestige and to the theatrical effect: small wonder that in the proclamations and Banns of York and Chester handsome costume was coupled with good acting and clear speech as the main attractions of the production:

> good players well arayed & openly spekyng
> (*REED York*, p. 25)

> Good speeche fine playes with Apparell comlye
> (*REED Chester*, p. 242).

Figure 3: *A 'prophets cappe' and a 'disciplis wede', two stock designs which appear to have changed very little over the years. From a Book of Hours printed by Vérard in 1487 (BL 1A 40846).*

The Shipwrights' Craft

Richard Beadle

This chapter considers an episode from the York cycle of mystery plays in relation to the everyday activity of the craft-guild which had responsibility for it. The play is no. VIII in the cycle, the Shipwrights', in which Noah is called upon by God to build the ark, and a representation of a vessel takes shape before the audience's eyes. How this feat was accomplished, and what the medieval audience saw is not evident from the text, nor is there any documentary information in the civic archives at York which might help to reconstruct the action. What the text does reveal, however, is that the actor playing Noah was called upon to describe and demonstrate, using quite technical language, several aspects of the medieval shipwright's craft. Noah is at once the ancient biblical patriarch and a contemporary York craftsman, and his ark is intended to be seen by the audience as both the huge symbolic vessel imagined by the biblical exegetes, and as a piece of local craftsmanship which the Shipwrights' guild and the city could be proud of. The play is a striking illustration of one of the major underlying concepts of the mystery cycles: as they phrased it then, the cycles were performed 'to the greater glory of God, and the profit and increase of the city'.[1] The dramatist who provided the York Shipwrights with their script – and he must have familiarized himself with a number of technical points in their trade before putting pen to parchment – gave them a play which did equal justice both to the grand symbolic trend of God's redemptive scheme, and to the skills employed by the guildsmen in their daily work. The Shipwrights' craft acquires a sacral significance through its ancient role in the divine ordering of things.

The Building of the Ark and the Flood were amongst a number of dramatically intractable subjects, like the Creation, or the drowning of Pharaoh's host in the Red Sea, undertaken by the medieval playwrights because of their great symbolic significance. Plays involving Noah were evidently popular and widespread in the later Middle Ages. Texts survive in the Towneley Manuscript (associated with Wakefield), in the N-Town collection (probably from East Anglia), in the Chester cycle, in a single survivor from the lost Newcastle cycle, and in the Cornish drama of the period. References in documents suggest that other places also had Noah plays, or at least tableaux-vivants involving the ark, amongst them Beverley, Dublin, Hereford, Hull, Lincoln and Norwich. Such presentations were nearly always mounted by guilds of shipwrights, carpenters, mariners or watermen. Anna Mill has shown that the example of Hull is particularly important.[2] The town evidently had no mystery cycle, but its mariners' guild staged a Noah play annually, involving a ship on wheels representing the ark. Detailed documentary accounts relating to the construction of the 'ark' and the staging of the play have survived from between 1461 and 1545, and as we shall see, they throw interesting light on the authentic character of the technical language employed by the York Shipwrights' playwright.

There are illuminating recent surveys of the Noah plays by Rosemary Woolf and Richard Axton.[3] They dramatize the events narrated in Genesis vi–viii, often with an admixture of apocryphal and legendary matter, particularly in the treatment of Noah's shrewish wife:

> The sorwe of Noe with his felaweshipe
> Er that he myghte gete his wyf to shipe
> (*Canterbury Tales*, A, 3539–40)

as Chaucer, who in the Miller's Tale shows his familiarity with Noah in contemporary drama, puts it. The importance of the episode in the scheme of the cycles emerges through the various ways in which its characters and incidents were interpreted as symbolic adumbrations of Christ, his ministry, his passion, his Church and many other features of Christian doctrine. The story of Noah was believed to foreshadow that of Christ, his ark was in some respects thought to prefigure the cross, and in others the Church. The Flood was held to look forward to the sacrament of baptism, and Noah's recalcitrant wife on the one hand repeated the disobedience of Eve, but on the other was looked on as a type of the Virgin in her eventual submission to God's will. These and many other symbolical Christian interpretations of the Old Testament story were in common currency in the later medieval period, and indeed received their widest dissemination through the popular drama and art of the time.

The York cycle is unique amongst the extant dramatic treatments of the Noah story in its division of the biblical material into two plays, the Shipwrights' 'Building of the Ark' and the Fishers' and Mariners' 'Flood'. The separating off of the 'Building of the Ark' suggests that it had a special significance which the original designers or organizers of the cycle wished to emphasize. The Shipwrights' play is perhaps at first sight the slightest of the extant Noah plays, running to only 151 lines, involving only two characters, and apparently containing nothing much in the way of dramatically arresting or attractive incident. God appears and explains that he proposes to drown everybody but Noah and his family in a universal flood, on account of the irretrievably sinful nature of the world. He gives Noah detailed instructions on how to build a boat, and Noah enacts the putting of them into effect, explaining some of the *minutiae* of contemporary shipbuilding to the audience at the same time. Whilst this is going on it appears that the prefabricated sections of the ark are brought together around him. One of the dramatic functions of Noah's 'technical' speech was probably to hold the audience's attention and 'cover' the action being carried on around him, perhaps by supernumeraries, or possibly by mechanical means. Towards the end of the play God appears again to see that his work has been carried out, and to give Noah further instructions as to the vessel's internal arrangements, and how it is to be loaded. Noah closes the play with a brief prayer calling for God's blessing on himself and the audience.

The style of the verse is plain, and well-adapted to its purpose. The dramatist was not tempted by the extremely elaborate alliterative stanzas used in many of the York plays, and adopted a simple octave in alternate rhymes, with sufficient decorative alliteration to give a pleasing balance and a brisk movement to the line. Most of the stanzas have a heavy pause at the mid-point, at the end of the fourth line. There is some intelligent use of the rhetorical device of *concatenatio*, whereby the last line of each stanza is echoed in the first line of the one following, yielding a mild form of wordplay. As we shall see, there is also wit (in the form of puns), some adroit use of epideictic syntax in the speeches of God and Noah concerning shipbuilding, and skilful deployment of diction and literary allusion. At the centre of the play's dramatic life is an attractive blend of humour and wonder, humour in the way in which God's staggering and peremptory command bewilders the massively aged and unsuspecting patriarch, wonder in the way in which the obedience of the old man generates a sudden access of grace, transforming him into a skilled craftsman whose one hundred years of work on the ark are completed in the passage of twenty lines of verse. These points are illustrated in the passages quoted below.

It is unfortunate that we know virtually nothing in detail about how the play was staged. The view that the York plays were staged processionally on pageant-wagons moving from station to station around the city is widely accepted. It may be that the Shipwrights had a wagon adapted to receive a superstructure representing the ark, but how the process of construction which evidently went forward in performance was actually achieved is a matter for speculation. Whatever happened, near the end of the play God is able to congratulate Noah on 'his' handiwork, and Noah goes off to see about loading 'my ship'. We are equally ignorant of the physical disposition of the two actors in relation to one another – whether, for instance, God appeared beside Noah, or whether he spoke from a higher level, as was certainly the case in other York plays, where we have stage-directions or documentary evidence to show how divine interventions in human affairs were managed.

The passage quoted at length below covers the central episode of the play, the actual construction of the ark. It is preceded by a speech addressed by God to the audience, in which he explains how he created the world for man, but how man, through the fall, became sinful. Now, he says, he intends to 'wirke þis werke . . . al newe' (24) having destroyed sinful mankind by drowning. Only the righteous Noah, and, for his sake, his family, will be spared. With this, God suddenly appears to Noah with the news that he must perform 'A warke to saffe þiselfe wythall' (35). The startled Noah is swiftly and amusingly characterized through the concessive and subordinate constructions he employs in his polite reply (41–4):

A, lorde, I lowe þe lowde and still	*praise*
Þat vnto me – wretche vnworthye –	
Þus with thy worde, as is þi will,	
Lykis to appere þus propyrly.	*in person*

Having arrested Noah's attention with his startling appearance, God wastes no time in conveying his no less surprising message (45–8):

Nooe, as I byd þe, doo fulfill:	
A shippe I will haue wroght in hye;	*quickly*
All-yf þou can litill skyll,	*even though*
Take it in hande, for helpe sall I.	

With more polite expressions Noah cautiously draws God's attention to his extreme old age and infirmity – later we learn he is 500 years old (49–52):

A, worthy lorde, wolde þou take heede,	
I am full olde and oute of qwarte	*unfit*
Þat me liste do no daies dede	*I am disinclined to do a day's*
Bot yf gret mystir me garte.	*work, unless urgent need force it upon me.*

The colloquial expression 'daies dede', day's work, in Noah's reply is important. It stands in a thread of diction running through the play from the very first line, 'First qwen I wrought þis world so wyde', recalling the works of the days of creation, and the idea of God as a divine artificer or craftsman. This idea is kept in the minds of the audience throughout the first 50 or so lines of the play by the repetition of the verb 'work':

Bot wirke þis werke I wille al newe (24)

is the expression used by God when he resolves to destroy the world and create anew. He echoes it in his first words to Noah, intimating the construction of the ark:

> I wyll þou wyrke withowten weyn
> A warke to saffe þiselfe wythall. (35–6)

'Work' as a noun also appears in lines 18 (= God's creation) and 53 (= the ark which is to be built), but of even more frequent occurrence is the verb in its old preterite or past participle form. God uses it in his opening line:

> Fyrst qwen I wrought þis world so wyde (1)

and on five further occasions before line 50 (9, 13, 18, 25), on the last applying it to the construction of the ark:

> A shippe I will haue wroght in hye (46).   *quickly*

'Make/made' also contributes to the effect:

> And to my likenes made I man (6)

and is the object of a quibble in the *concatenatio* between the second and third stanzas:

> . . . me repentys and rewys forþi   *I therefore repent and regret*
> Þat ever I made outhir man or wiffe.   *either*

> Bot sen they make me to repente
> My werke I wrought so wele and trewe (15–18).

The dramatist, in short, has saturated his verse with words emphasizing the idea of God as a worker, a craftsman who makes tangible objects, and it is in the making of a divinely ordained artifact that God conveys his skill to Noah at the heart of the play. The words 'work/wrought', 'craft' and 'make/making' are prominent throughout this passage. It is also conspicuous for its use of unusual technical terms from shipwrightry, and a brief glossary of these will be found in the Appendix.

> [*Deus*] I se suche ire emonge mankynde
> Þat of þare wèrkis I will take wreke;
> Þay shall be sownkyn for þare synne,
> Þerfore a shippe I wille þou make.   60
> Þou and þi sonnes shall be þerein,
> They sall be sauyd for thy sake.
> Therfore go bowdly and begynne
> Thy mesures and thy markis to take.

> *Noe* A, lorde, þi wille sall euer be wroght   65
> Os counsill gyfys of ilka clerk,
> Bot first, of shippe-craft can I right noght;
> Of þer makyng haue I no merke.
> *Deus* Noe, I byd þe hartely haue no þought,
> I sall þe wysshe in all þi werke,   70
> And even to itt till ende be wroght;
> Therefore to me take hede and herke.

54

God: I see so much sinful turmoil amongst mankind that I will wreak vengeance upon their deeds. They shall be drowned because of their sin, and therefore I command you to build a ship. You and your sons shall take refuge on board – they shall be saved for your sake. Now go briskly and take note of your measurements and dimensions.
Noah: Ah, Lord, every learned man counsels that your will must always be done. But in the first place, I know nothing about shipwrightry, I have no idea how to build boats. *God*: Noah, earnestly I advise you, do not be concerned, I shall guide you in all your work, until you have completely finished it – therefore listen to me, and pay attention.

The calculated repetition of words like 'work' and 'make' in this and the following passages is now supplemented by the use of terms in specialized senses connected with woodwork and shipbuilding. God tells the as yet unskilled Noah to go and begin taking his 'mesures' and 'markis', but Noah replies that he knows nothing of 'shippe-crafte', obliquely reminding the audience of the guild responsible for the play they are watching. In the biblical narrative of these events (Genesis vi. 13–16), Noah of course engages in no conversation with God. God's instructions become more specific, and the dramatist continues to draw on the technical vocabulary of shipbuilding in his own day to depict exactly how God teaches Noah his craft:

> Take high trees and hewe þame cleyne,
>   All be sware and noght of skwyn,
> Make of þame burdes and wandes betwene   75
>   Þus thrivandly, and noght ouer-thyn.
> Luke þat þi semes be suttilly seyn
>   And naylid wele þat þei noght twyne;
> Þus I deuyse ilk dele bedeyne,
>   Þerfore do furthe, and leue thy dyne.   80
>
> iij C cubyttis it sall be lang,
>   And fyfty brode, all for thy blys;
> Þe highte, of thyrty cubittis strang,
>   Lok lely þat þou thynke on þis.
> Þus gyffe I þe grathly or I gang   85
>   Þi mesures, þat þou do not mysse.
> Luk nowe þat þou wirke noght wrang
>   Þus wittely sen I þe wyshe.

Select tall trees, and cut the timber in a neat fashion, squarely, not on a slant. Make them into boards, (?) with laths to go between them, in a satisfactory manner – let them not be too thin. Take care that your seams are properly attended to, and nailed securely so that they do not come apart. This is how I plan that everything should be, so proceed with the work, and do not complain. The ship will be 300 cubits long and 50 wide, for your convenience. The height will be fully thirty cubits – make sure that you consider this faithfully. I have carefully given you these measurements before I go, so that you do not make any mistake. Take care that you work accurately, since I am instructing you so wisely.

God begins by telling Noah how to cut down trees and dress the timber in such a way as to produce 'burdes' and 'wandes' for the hull of the boat. He emphasizes that the wood should be cut with, not across the grain. He draws particular attention to the accurate alignment and securing of the 'semes', the gaps between the planks which make up the hull. The measurements given in the second stanza just quoted derive directly from Genesis, though few of the audience can have had any idea of what a cubit was. (It was in fact 'an ancient measure of length derived from the forearm; varying at different times and places, but usually about 18–22 inches' *OED* sb.2.) Noah, as if suddenly divinely inspired, goes on to put the instructions into action:

Noe	A, blistfull lord, þat al may beylde,	
	I thanke þe hartely both euer and ay;	90
	Fyfe hundreth wyntres I am of elde –	
	Methynk þer ȝeris as yestirday.	
	Ful wayke I was and all vnwelde,	
	My werynes is wente away,	
	To wyrk þis werke here in þis feylde	95
	Al be myselfe I will assaye.	
	To hewe þis burde I wyll begynne,	
	But firste I wille lygge on my lyne;	
	Now bud it be alle inlike thynne,	
	So þat it nowthyr twynne nor twyne.	100
	Þus sall I june it with a gynn	
	And sadly sett it with symonde fyne:	
	Þus schall I wyrke it both more and mynne	
	Thurgh techyng of God, maistir myne.	

Noah: Ah, heavenly Lord, who may succour all, I thank you sincerely, for ever and ever. I am five hundred years old, but now these years seem as yesterday to me. I used to be quite weak and feeble, but now my weariness has vanished. By myself I shall now undertake this work.

I will begin by cutting this board, but first I will lay my measuring line on it. It must be of the same thickness as others so that when joined it will neither come apart nor warp. Thus shall I fix it in place with this tool and make it firm with good cement. In this way I proceed with the work in every respect according to the guidance of God my master.

Here we see Noah setting to work with his (measuring) 'lyne', ensuring that the planks for the hull are of equal thickness, joining them, and, it appears, caulking the seam between them with a substance which he describes as 'symonde', or cement. This is probably intended to stand for the 'pitch' which God tells Noah to use in the biblical account (Genesis vi. 14). Noah goes on to display to the audience other objects used by the medieval shipbuilder:

[. . .   . . .]
   More suttelly kan no man sewe;   105
It sall be cleyngked euerilka dele
   With nayles þat are both noble and newe.
Þus sall I feste it fast to feele.
   Take here a revette, and þere a rewe,
With þer þe bowe nowe wyrke I wele;   110
   Þis werke I warand both gud and trewe.

Full trewe it is who will take tente,
   Bot faste my force begynnes to fawlde.
A hundereth wyntres away is wente
   Sen I began þis werk, full grathely talde,   115
And in slyke trauayle for to be bente
   Is harde to hym þat is þus olde.
But he þat to me þis messages sent
   He wille be my beylde, þus am I bowde.

Deus   Nooe, þis werke is nere an ende   120
         And wrought right as I warned þe.

. . . no man can sew more skilfully. It shall be clenched throughout with good, new nails – thus shall I be sure to build it soundly. Here I place a rivet, and there a rove, (?) with these I now skilfully shape the bow. Certainly, this work is sound and accurate. So much is clear to anybody who will take heed, but now my strength is ebbing rapidly. A hundred winters have passed since I began this work, there is no doubt, and it is hard for one as old as me to labour in work of this kind. But I may make bold to say that he who gave me my instructions will continue to support me.
God: Noah, this work is almost finished, and you have executed it exactly as I told you . . .

The first of these stanzas contains the fundamental term of medieval shipbuilding, 'cleyngked', that is, clenched, or in modern boat-building terminology, clinkered. Noah shows the audience how the boards were nailed together with 'revette(s)', whose points, having passed through the wood, were turned over or flattened on metal plates with holes in them, known as roves ('rewe(s)'). This process was intended to prevent the nails from springing out when under pressure from the water when the vessel was afloat.

In northern Europe virtually all ships were clinker-built before the end of the fifteenth century. The process may be briefly described. A frame was laid down consisting of the keel and cross-ribs of the vessel, on to which were nailed the strakes, rows of horizontal overlapping planks, which went to form the hull. The seams, which were the gaps between the planks, were caulked with oakum or tow, and sealed with pitch or resin. As far as the manner of construction goes, the play discussed here presents the ark as a medieval boat, and both its designer and its builder as medieval ship-wrights. In the case of Noah the boat-builder, such a conception was not uncommon and it is sometimes found in depictions of the building of the ark in illustrated manuscripts of the period. For instance Cambridge, St. John's College, MS. K. 26 (a thirteenth-century English psalter) contains an illustration of Noah working on his boat with a tool clearly recognizable as an auger (see plate 4). Oxford, Bodleian Library, MS. Bodley 270b (a thirteenth-century French *Bible Moralisée*) has a picture of the ark under construction in a medieval shipyard, with Noah using an axe, another craftsman a drill, and a third caulking the seams with a spoon.[4] The same tradition is reflected in the play, but what is also remarkable is the play-wright's insistence on the idea of God actually teaching Noah the craft which he goes on to display to the audience.

The copious and demonstrative use of technical terms has an air of self-conscious authenticity about it. It is interesting to note that the docu-mentary records of the Hull Noah play printed by Anna Mill have some of the same terms (and many others) applied to the construction and repair of the ship which went about the town: 'clenkyng', the basic term in medieval shipbuilding, occurs repeatedly.[5] One suspects that the actor playing Noah at York was equipped with various properties which might in fact have been supplied by the Shipwrights' guild: suitably shaped pieces of wood, cutting and drilling tools, 'cement', rivets and roves, a measuring line.[6] God's practical tone in giving instructions (the repeated 'þus . . .' in lines 76, 79 and 85) is echoed by Noah when he sets to work ('þus . . .' in 101, 103 and 108); and God having withdrawn, Noah's speech was doubtless directed demonstratively to the audience ('who will take tente', 112).

These are some of the means whereby the dramatist creates a link between the daily labour of the York Shipwrights and the parts played by God and their remote ancestor Noah in the drama of salvation. But a distinctly odd feature of the passage must also be noted. Noah's practical shipwrightry as shown in the play is of a fairly limited nature, whereas God's instructions to him faithfully reproduce the biblical requirements for a massive vessel, i.e. one with a displacement of some 40,000 tons. Whether or not the dramatist and his audience were aware of exactly how large a ship 300 cubits long, 50 broad and 30 high would have been in reality, it is clear that the biblical dimensions of the ark have been retained for reasons other than the literal. Even more palpably preposterous is Noah's claim in lines 114–15, to the effect that 100 years have passed since he began work in line 95. It is important, however, to recall that a second level of meaning resides in many of the detailed references to the ark and its construction, including some of the technical terms. Reference has been made above to the general spiritual significance of the Noah story in medieval exegesis of the bible. Patristic writers devoted minute attention

Plate 4: *The Building of the Ark (St. John's College, Cambridge, MS K. 26, f 7v.). Noah has removed his hood and cloak (which lie on the ground) and works on the Ark with an auger.*

to every detail in the building of the ark, finding in it prefigurations of episodes in the life of Christ, and symbols of Christian doctrine and of the Church. These are too numerous to examine in detail here, and examples must suffice.[7] The ark was commonly likened to the Church: as there was only one ark, so there is only one Church, the sole refuge from certain destruction. The fact that it was made of wood naturally led to the suggestion that it prefigured the cross, perhaps glanced at in God's reference here to 'high trees' (73), 'tree' being commonly used in Middle English to signify the cross. Numerology was much cultivated, and the figures given for the dimensions of the ark were seized upon eagerly – for instance, the thirty cubits in height were likened to the thirty years of Christ's life on earth, or alternatively, the thirty books of the Old and New Testaments. The fact that Noah's work took one hundred years – casually referred to in the play, but disconcerting to the literal expectations of a modern audience – was allegorized as the period of grace, and indeed Noah is seen to receive a sudden access of supernatural assistance as he begins work (91–4). The grace which makes his 500 years seem as yester-day is perhaps a comparable force to that acting on the audience of the play, where 100 years are made to pass in twenty lines. Even small technical details were given allegorical significance. God's instruction to dress his timber 'All be sware' (74) was held to look forward to the heavenly city of the apocalypse, which stands four-square. The material used for securing the seams of the vessel – probably the 'symonde' men-tioned by Noah in the play (102) – was referred to the human soul, as the binding power of love.

These and other symbolic aspects of the ark and its construction would have been for the most part accessible only to the learned members of the audience. As we have seen, the dramatist sought to engage the attention of the bulk of the audience on another level. This ability to appeal to different levels of assent in an audience is often a mark of skill in dramatic poetry, and the evidence for the York dramatist's ability in this direction may be readily elaborated. The speeches quoted above are also allusive in other ways, and are by no means without wit. For example, when God says to Noah of his family 'They sall be sauyd *for thy sake* (62)' he alludes to the biblical reason why Noah in particular was selected as the instrument of salvation, the second father of mankind, being the one righteous man who 'walked with God', 'perfect in his generation' (Genesis vi, 9). Noah's submissive response, 'A, lorde, *þi wille* sall euer *be wroght*' (65) slips into the supplicatory mode of the Lord's Prayer, *fiat voluntas tua*, 'thy will be done'. Another form of verbal interplay revolves around the word 'mark'. In line 64 God instructs Noah to go and begin work by taking 'markis', measurements, of the wood. Noah wryly picks up the word in his reply (67–8) and alters the sense, he knows nothing of 'shippe-crafte', of the making of boats he has no 'merke', i.e. knowledge, understanding (*MED*, marke(e n. (1), 11. (b) quotes this example).

The closing lines of the play are graced by an even more adroit pun which draws together many of the conceptual issues brought out in the preceding pages. Having received further instructions from God as to the construction of the inside of the ark, and the need to get the animals and his family on board, Noah closes the play by invoking a blessing on himself and on the audience of the play:

> He þat to me þis Crafte has kende   *made known*
> He wysshe vs with his worthy wille.   *guide*
> (150–1)

The divine inspiration of Noah's skill in shipwrightry, and by implication the divine origin of the York Shipwrights' daily labour, is acknowledged in the primary sense of 'Crafte': skill, trade. 'Craft' in the sense of 'vessel' was a relatively late semantic development, though Olof Arngart has shown that a ship could be called a craft as early as the fourteenth century.[8] A more generalized sense was usual in Middle English: 'that which is constructed', an artifact; here, the ark (*MED*, craft n. (1), 9. (a)). The capital C which the word is given in the above quotation is in the manuscript, and it may perhaps have originated in a reminder to the actor preparing his part to stress the word or add a gesture. What is not in doubt was the dramatist's intention to leave his audience with a very rich idea of 'craft': God's, Noah's, and the York Shipwrights'.

'Heven and erthe in lytyl space'

Janet Cowen

Ther is no rose of swych vertu
As is the rose that bar Jhesu;
   Allelyua.

For in this rose conteynyd was
Heven and erthe in lytyl space,
   Res miranda.

The paradox of infinity contained in a finite space has often been used to give expression to the doctrine of the Incarnation. For the playwright, as for the visual artist, space is a primary medium. The writers of the mystery plays had as their subject a cosmic history articulating the central doctrines of the Christian faith. They had the opportunity to represent, in the particular space of the playing area, the communication between the divine and the human, the bounding and containing of the infinite, which is implied in the doctrine of the Incarnation.

The question of the original staging of mystery plays is, of course, still largely a matter for judicious speculation. Increasingly we can enjoy the benefit of having available in well edited modern collections (the *REED* and Malone Society volumes) those contemporary records which hint at some of the practical details of the play performances. But, except for certain antiquarian writings which post-date the original performances, the records do not anticipate the concerns of those who now take the keenest interest in them. They are largely the work-a-day papers of the civic authorities and trade guilds responsible for organizing and putting on the plays. Their compilers were making up minutes and balancing accounts, not writing theatrical reviews. The information they give is necessarily selective, often fragmentary, sometimes cryptic, and usually open to more than one interpretation, as Meg Twycross has already pointed out in her discussion of costume.

In attempting an imaginative reconstruction of the late medieval playwright's use of space we have to draw inferences from two kinds of evidence, each in its way obscure: the records and the play texts themselves. A theatre historian a few hundred years hence who was trying to imagine the original staging of a twentieth century play of which no photographs or reviews had survived might at least find a sound basis in an acting edition of the text. But, as Peter Meredith has shown in Chapter 2, in the case of the mystery plays the indications are that most of the manuscripts which have survived, although they include here and there stage directions which may well be original, are not acting texts themselves, but copies made for various different purposes.

We must bear this in mind as we consider the selection of material in the plays, the inferences of the dialogue and the stated or implied action, and try to appreciate the potential dramatic effect. Experiment is the best method of discovery, of course, and there has been an increasing opportunity in recent years to see productions of the plays in different settings and circumstances.

The distribution of material into individual plays varies significantly from cycle to cycle in a way which carries both thematic emphasis and implications for staging. In the Towneley and York cycles, for example, the Annunciation and the Nativity form the main subjects of separate plays. In the Chester cycle they are both contained within one play, together with a substantial amount of other material. In N-Town they are in separate plays, but as items in a more complex compilation of material (see table on p. 64).

The York plays of the Annunciation and Nativity seem to be very economical in the use of space, and each episode has a single visual focus. Here the subjects under discussion are more clearly divided than in the other cycles into discrete units, into separate plays, in fact, assigned to different guilds. The Spicers' Play deals with the Annunciation and the Visit to Elizabeth, episodes which follow one another in Luke's Gospel. The Visit to Elizabeth takes place, realistically speaking, in another location, but the frequent concurrence of the Annunciation and Visitation as a double subject in medieval visual art[1] may provide, by analogy, a convention which would make acceptable the staging of these two scenes in close proximity to one another, on the same platform. Joseph's Doubts form the subject of a separate play. The story of Joseph's dismay at Mary's pregnancy, his resolve to leave her and his change of heart when her miraculous conception is explained to him by an angel in a dream, is based ultimately on Matthew i.19. It is developed here, as elsewhere, in terms borrowed from the fabliau theme of the incompatibility of an old husband and a young wife. The emphasis of the York play is personal and domestic. The only characters apart from Joseph and Mary are the two maidservants whom Joseph reproaches for not having kept a proper eye on Mary while he was away. They contribute to the argument by taking Mary's part, and

N-TOWN

(*8, 9, 10* The Conception of Mary, Mary in the Temple, The Marriage of Joseph and Mary)

11

1–32	prayer of Contemplation
33–216	Parliament of Heaven
217–340	Annunciation

12
Joseph's doubts

13

1–20	Joseph and Mary plan to visit Elizabeth
21–42	Contemplation's speech introducing Elizabeth and Zakarie
43–152	visit to Elizabeth

Concluding speech of Contemplation

Speech of Den the Summoner

14
The Trial of Joseph and Mary

15

1–55	Journey to Bethlehem
56–88	dialogue with citizen
89–124	Joseph and Mary in stable
125–168	Joseph fetches midwives
169–320	miracle of midwife's hand

TOWNELEY

Explicit pharao
Incipit Cesar Augustus

1–36	Emperor boasts his power
37–126	Emperor consults counsellors; Sirin sent for
127–39	Messenger goes to Sirin
140–204	Sirin goes to Emperor and advises him
205–40	Messenger sent out to announce tax

Explicit Cesar Augustus
Incipit Annunciacio

1–76	God's prologue
77–154	Annunciation
155–373	Joseph's doubts

Explicit Annunciacio beate Marie

Incipit Salutacio Elezabeth

1–90	visit to Elizabeth

Explicit Salutacio Elezabeth
Incipit Pagina pastorum

YORK

The Spicers

1–144	Prologue, recalling fall of man and prophets and introducing Annunciation
145–96	Annunciation
197–240	visit to Elizabeth

The Pewterers and Founders

1–74	Joseph complains alone
75–235	dialogue: Joseph, attendants, Mary
236–89	Joseph and angel
290–305	Joseph and Mary

The Tilethatchers

1–44	Joseph and Mary at the stable
45–70	Mary alone
71–83	Joseph outside stable
84–154	Joseph and Mary address the child

CHESTER

The Wrightes Playe

Pagina Sexta, De Salutatione et Nativitate Salvatoris Jesu Christi

1–48	Annunciation
49–120	meeting with Elizabeth
121–76	Joseph's doubts
177–344	Octavian arranges taxing; Senators come to Octavian
345–72	Octavian consults Sibyl
373–420	Herald announces tax
421–52	Joseph and Mary set out to Bethlehem; vision of glad and sorry people
453–76	Joseph and Mary arrive at the stable
477–500	Joseph fetches midwives
501–63	Joseph and Mary greet the child; miracle of the midwife's hand
564–643	Expositor's account of the miraculous destruction of the Temple of Peace
644–98	Sibyl announces the birth of Christ; Octavian's vision and offering of incense
699–722	Expositor's conclusion

their presence provides an appropriately domestic frame of reference for the small marital comedy which is acted out in this play. The play ends with the preparations for the journey to Bethlehem. Joseph tells Mary to put their belongings in a pack, saying, 'Helpe vp nowe on my bak', and they presumably leave as if to go on their way. The break between this play and the next covers the journey, the next play opening with their arrival at the stable. Joseph's opening lines imply that they have been seeking for shelter elsewhere:

> For we haue sought both vppe and doune
> Thurgh diuerse stretis in þis cité.
>
> (8–9)

In processional staging, where this play occupied the location vacated by the previous one, this illusion would be very easy to create: the actors for this play could simply move into view of the audience at a particular station, having walked along the street. The confined setting of a wagon stage also seems appropriate for this play. The action of the play is focused on the stable. The play is notable for the way it combines realism and intimacy with formality and devotion. Joseph's opening speech immediately creates a particular mood and setting. He speaks of the bad weather, the dilapidated condition of the stable, and their great weariness. Then he goes away to fetch light, leaving all attention focused on Mary. In the lines that follow she speaks of the imminent birth, and then she greets the newly born child in a formal and reverent speech. Modern productions have managed this apparently awkward point of dramatic obstetrics by various devices,[2] none that I have come across being, in my view, very satisfactory. I think that the moment could probably be managed quite simply, and that a clue to it may be found in the literary and visual sources which are recognized as lying behind the York play. From the late fourteenth century onwards, visual representations of the Nativity show the influence of the *Revelations* of St Bridgit,[3] an account of the experience of the widely known and influential Swedish visionary. Her account includes a vision of the birth of Christ in which she saw the Virgin kneeling in prayer and the child, naked and shining with light, suddenly appear on the ground before her. Copies of the text of the *Revelations* were widely disseminated, even before the Saint's death, and there are several English versions from the fifteenth century.[4] It seems clear that the York play of the Nativity is indebted, either directly or indirectly, to the *Revelations* for its selection and ordering of material.[5] Points of identity include the restriction of the persons in the scene to Joseph and Mary, Joseph's absence during the birth, the Virgin's reverent address to the child, her taking the child on her lap (implied in the play by Joseph's exclamation on his return: 'O Marie! what swete thyng is þat on thy kne?'), Joseph's amazement and awe, and the worship of the child by Mary and Joseph together, with which both the vision and the play conclude.

Early pictorial representations of the vision include details mentioned in St. Bridgit's account, such as the mantle and shoes laid aside by the Virgin, and the clothes put out in preparation for dressing the child, and some also include the watching figure of the Saint herself. These details are lost in later tradition, but the characteristic kneeling position of the Virgin, and the naked child on the ground, are frequently found. This new icono-graphical pattern replaced an older scheme in which the Virgin was usually shown in a bed with the child in the manger beside her. There are numerous woodcuts in English books of the late fifteenth and early six-teenth centuries which are modelled on this new popular pattern (see plate 5).[6] Some of these have additional figures, angels and shepherds being a frequent later variant, some have only the figures of Mary and Joseph, as in the York play. In many of them the child is lying not on the bare ground but on a corner of the long cloak which the Virgin is wearing, a frequent variant in North European examples. This suggests a way in which the birth could have been very conveniently represented on stage. It would be easy for a doll to be concealed in the folds of a long cloak looped over the fore-arm. After the lines announcing the birth the actor could simply kneel, spread out the cloak so that the doll lay on one corner of it, and immediately be in the posture of adoration required by the lines which follow. Whether or not the audience knew of the Brigittine tradition that the Virgin gave birth while kneeling in prayer, the moment would be lent both credibility and decorum by assimilation to a familiar visual image.

The York play of the Nativity has been greatly admired for its economy, its clearly focused visual impression, its intimacy, its simple dignity and its control of tone. Some of the praise it has received has been given in the light of modern revivals of the play, which have been staged in a variety of settings. Despite the abundance of dramatic records from York, there is still considerable disagreement about the original staging and setting.[7] Whether or not a processional method of staging for this cycle can be proved beyond reasonable doubt, the three plays under consideration, in their compactness and dramatic concentration, seem very well suited to that type of presentation.

The Chester Wrights' Play, on the other hand, is ambitious in scope, and somewhat varied in method and tone. It opens with a brief and simple Annunciation whose dialogue follows the familiar Gospel outline. After the concluding stanza of the scene, in which Mary gives her assent to the angel's message, a stage direction follows, indicating the departure of the angel and the meeting of Mary and Elizabeth: *Tunc Angelus ibit, et Maria salutabit Elizabeth*.[8] The dialogue continues with Mary's greeting. Although neither the stage direction nor the dialogue indicates exactly what is to be done, movement of some kind is clearly called for here, for Elizabeth's later suggestion that they return to Joseph (lines 113–16) implies that Mary has travelled from home to see her. On their arrival Joseph exclaims at Mary's condition, and there follows the scene in which he resolves to leave her. Joseph is so depressed by the business that he says he must sleep, and while he does so the angel appears to him to assure him of Mary's innocence. It seems obvious that at some point, either before or after the appearance of the angel to Joseph, Elizabeth, at least, must withdraw, since she has no further part in the play. Whether Mary remains behind, although she does not speak, and whether she and Joseph now remain in view of the audience, is not specified. In what follows, however, the audience's attention is directed away from them to a new set of characters, as there bursts in upon the scene the Emperor Octavian's herald, announcing the appearance of the Emperor himself. The words used suggest that the entrance could be made through the audience:

> Make rowme, lordinges, and give us waye
> and lett Octavian come and playe
>
> (177–8).

Octavian addresses the assembled company, in English and French, speaking of his pre-eminence in power, and announcing his plan for taking of tax of a penny a head as a means both of exerting his authority and of calculating its extent. Something to represent a palace, or at least a throne, seems needed for this scene, as is possibly implied in the lines:

> for soe dreade a duke sate never on dayes   *dais*
> in Rome
>
> (239–40).

Octavian dispatches his messenger to announce the tax. Then senators arrive to visit him, sent by the Romans to honour him as a god. Octavian shows scruples about accepting the homage due to a deity, and consults the Sibyl, asking her if there will ever be any earthly king to surpass him. The Sibyl tells him that a child is to be born who will be eternal; she cannot yet tell him when, but when she sees any ghostly signs she will warn him. Then follows a stage direction sending both the Sibyl and the herald about their business, the Sibyl to prayer, the herald to proclaim the tax: *Tunc orat Sibilla, et dicat Preco alta voce*. The proclamation is overheard by Joseph, so distracting the audience's attention back to him. But again there seems no need to assume that the characters from the preceding scene should withdraw altogether. The dialogue requires that Octavian depart from Sibyl, but she might remain visible, at prayer, during the following scenes. Joseph listens to the summons to go to Bethlehem to be taxed. Mary must be with him, or within call, since he now speaks to her as he prepares to set out on the journey, taking an ox and ass with him to sell. Whether live

animals were used in the Chester plays is a point on which the records offer
tantalizingly contradictory hints. It seems clear, in any case, that the ass
here must carry Mary, for on their arrival at Bethlehem she asks Joseph to
help her down. The intervening journey might most conveniently be staged
at ground level, for the scope of the scene enlarges suddenly, and requires
the introduction of a crowd. As they travel, Mary exclaims at the sight of
two groups of people, one glad and merry, the other sighing and sorry. The
meaning of the vision is explained to her by an angel: the glad people are
those who will see Christ's coming; the sad are the Jews, who will not
recognize Christ. Although it would be economical in terms of space and
casting to use the audience for these people,[9] that might, given the
interpretation, be a rather risky way to deploy a medieval crowd. But
perhaps the audience might more easily be brought into play a few
moments later to represent the second crowd required by this scene, the
crowd in Bethlehem, which Joseph remarks on as he and Mary approach
the place which represents the stable:

> Marye, suster, sooth to saye
> harbour I hope gett wee ne maye;
> for great lordes of stowte araye
> occupye this cyttye.
> Therfore wee muste in good faye
> lye in this stable tyll yt bee daye.
> (453–58)

Following Mary's request to him to help her down are stage directions
indicating that he should take her in his arms and place her between the ox
and the ass: *Tunc Joseph accipiet Mariam in brachia sua. Tunc statuet
Mariam inter bovem et asinam.* In the next few lines Joseph leaves to fetch
midwives.

   In the following lines Joseph meets the midwives and takes them back to
the stable. Mary welcomes him back, but implies she will need no
assistance:

> But God will worke of his power
> full sonne for mee,
> (498–500).

There is a stage direction, *Tunc paululum acquiescunt* ('Then they keep
silence a while'), and then Mary shows Joseph the child:

> A, Joseph, tydinges aright!
> I have a sonne, a sweete wight . . .
> commen hee is here in this sight
> Godes Sonne, as thow maye see.
> (501–8).

A stage direction then indicates the appearance of the star: *Tunc stella
apparebit.*

Plate 5: *The Nativity, from Simon, the Anker of London Wall*, The Fruyte of Redempcyon, *A5 v (BL C21 c23)*.

The sequence of the dialogue seems clearly to require that, as in the York play, the actual moment of birth should form part of the scene, and the discreet stage direction, *Tunc paululum acquiescunt*, seems to provide for this moment without making it clear what dramatic convention was to be adopted. Although this play differs from the York play of the Nativity in including the tradition of the midwives and in having Joseph present at the birth, it requires a similar effect at this point, and the suggestion offered above for York could meet the case here too.

The Chester play then continues with the scene in which the sceptical midwife tries to test Mary's virginity. Her hand is withered when she attempts to touch Mary in this spirit of doubt, but she is healed when, following the prompting of an angel, she begs mercy of the child.

At this point the character named Expositor speaks. This is the commentator who appears in the earlier play of Abraham to explain the significance of Melchizedeck's offering of bread and wine. He now reminds the audience that the withering and healing of the midwife's hand was not the only miracle that took place at Christ's birth, and he recounts the story

69

of a miraculous destruction of a temple in Rome. The playwright's immediate source for this apocryphal material, as for the miracle of the midwife's hand and the Sibyl's prophecy, is *A Stanzaic Life of Christ*,[10] a
vernacular Gospel harmony with commentaries for the laity which provides material for several parts of the cycle. The Expositor takes the tone
of the source as he impresses on the audience's attention the marvellous
nature of the events which accompanied Christ's birth in a quite lengthy
address (eighty lines) which refers, for the most part, to phenomena which
have no counterpart on stage. His concluding instances, however, refer
back to the dramatic situation:

> The oxe, the asse, ther they were lent,   *where ? dwelling*
> honored Christe in theyr intent;
> and moe miracles, as wee have ment
> to playe right here anon.
> (640–43)

The following lines redirect the audience's attention sharply to the Sibyl.
She has now seen the ghostly sign for which she has been waiting. A stage
direction indicates a move to the Emperor: *veniet Sibilla ad imperatorem*,
and she announces to him that the child is born who shall surpass all earthly
kings. She directs his attention to the vision which she herself sees, and
Octavian exclaims:

> A, Sibbell, this is a wondrouse sight,
> for yonder I see a mayden bright,
> a yonge chylde in her armes . . .
> (651–53)

He makes an offering of incense, during which the angel sings. It seems
that the senators, too, see the vision; one of them describes it as being
contained in the star:

> for in the stare, as thinkes mee,
> I see a full fayre maye.   *? maid*
> (693–94)

What they must surely be looking at is the stable, possibly appearing
illuminated in some way by the star.

The Expositor then refers to the church which the Emperor had built to
commemorate this moment, and brings the play to a conclusion with a final
vigorous reiteration of the moral of the midwife's hand:

> hyr hand roted, as you have seene,
> Wherby you may take good teene   *heed*
> that unbeleeffe is a fowle sinne,
> as you have seene within this playe
> (719–22).

What the audience has seen is this and much more besides. In terms of its materials and methods, and of its staging effects, the play is notable for its diversity. Its seven hundred and twenty two lines contain Biblical, apocryphal and invented material, comprising several incidents and expressed as dialogue, soliloquy, prayer, prophecy, vision and exposition. Its action requires exits, entrances, journeys, meetings, appearances, disappearances, singing, silence, crowds, light, animals, two supernatural visions, a withered hand and a healing miracle. It is not surprising that one critic has estimated it as 'singularly crowded and diffuse in its effect'.[11] But the diverse material is not without structure, and the structure of the play is related to the implied needs of its staging. It seems that for most effective staging of this play more than one raised platform is needed. The final scene, in which Octavian and his court see the vision of the Holy Family, suggests at least two. Something to represent Mary's house is needed for the Annunciation. Perhaps such a platform could also accommodate the Visit to Elizabeth, in accordance with the traditional pairing of the two subjects noted above. If it was vacated after Mary's return home and then re-used for the Octavian and Sibyl scenes a typological parallel could be nicely pointed: both the Annunciation and the Sibyl's prophecy dramatize the communication of supernatural knowledge. But with or without these conjectural economies, it seems dramatically desirable that there should be some physical separation between Rome and Bethlehem.

It is, of course, from Chester that we have the quite detailed, if somewhat problematic, description of movable wagon stages and their being wheeled in succession to various places in the city to provide continuous performances at these different stations. This is the description found in the compilations of the Chester historian, David Rogers, writing at the beginning of the seventeenth century. It has been often quoted and much discussed, and doubt has been cast on its reliability, as the author was probably never an eye-witness of the plays himself, although he may have been using manuscript sources dating from the last years of the plays' performance. Recent discussions of the staging of the Chester plays have, however, been inclined to treat Rogers' description with respect, despite the problems which remain in interpreting some of the detail. It has been strongly argued[12] that a performance staged at several stations, using movable wagon stages ('pageants', as Rogers terms them), would have been a feasible operation at Chester, given a certain interpretation of Rogers' naming of the stations and assuming some ancillary staging. It has been thought reasonable to assume that the wagon stages would be supplemented by other platforms or structures, which could even have been already in position at the stations where performance was to take place, thus making possible the simultaneous use of separate acting areas which several of the plays seem to demand. In the Wrights' Play, the Nativity itself takes place between the two Octavian scenes, and the stable must still be visible during the second of these scenes. A similar 'envelope' structure of scenes is found in other parts of the cycle.

The 'envelope' structuring of the Sibyl scenes (which does not derive from the source) gives the play considerable dramatic potential, a potential which derives from what at first sight might seem to make the play unwieldy, that is, the playwright's predilection for the miraculous. When the journey to Bethlehem and the Nativity are combined in this way with the Sibyl's prophecy, the play is advancing two separate narratives which are causally related. The Emperor's demand for tribute provides the motive for the journey to Bethlehem; the birth of the child provides the answer to Octavian's questions about his own status and is the fulfilment of the Sibyl's prophecy. The fulfilment of prophecy is, of course, an important theme in all the cycles, and arguably particularly so in the Chester cycle, with its extended treatment of the subject in the play of Balaam. The play of the Nativity dramatizes the theme in a particularly effective way. When the Sibyl shows to Octavian the miraculous vision which is a validation of her prophecy, what they are both looking at is the stage on which the audience has just seen the Nativity enacted. In this way, the audience's experience of the enacted event acts, in dramatic terms, as a corroboration of the miraculous appearance of that event in the Sibyl's vision. The audience knows that what she is seeing has happened. By this happy combination of scenes, prophecy and vision are articulated in the play's structure, the miraculous is demonstrated in its setting. Also demonstrated in the juxtaposition of these scenes is the contrast between earthly and heavenly power, a theme brought into sharp focus at the moment when the Emperor, who had demanded tribute as a demonstration of his authority, himself makes an offering of incense to the Christ child.

We must always bear in mind in thinking about the mystery plays that as the performances continued over the years there would have been changes. The guilds who were responsible for putting on the individual plays may sometimes have found it difficult to meet their commitments, and plays would have been modified or amalgamated. Conversely, in different circumstances, plays may have been expanded or split in two. There are indications in the records, and in some variation between the different play manuscripts, that this kind of modification went on in Chester.[13] Without yielding to the lure of hypothetical revisions, we must bear in mind that we are dealing with plays affected by changing circumstances of performance, and that some of the effects we observe may be the result of modifications to an existing idea. But whether or not the Wrights' Play contains revisions, it has a more purposeful structure than it has sometimes been credited with, a structure which has its counterparts in other plays of the cycle.

The corresponding subjects are treated in N-Town with very different selection and emphasis. Here there is a notable concentration of material about the early life of the Virgin. The play in which the Annunciation is presented is numbered 11 in the manuscript. Before this are three plays dealing respectively with the conception of Mary, her dedication to the temple in childhood, and her marriage to Joseph. The play of the conception of Mary tells the story, deriving from the apocryphal gospels, of how Joachim's offering in the Temple is refused because of the barrenness of his wife, Anna. Ashamed, he goes to live among shepherds in the country, and during this time an angel announces to Joachim and Anna in turn the news of the future birth of Mary. In this way, the conception of the Virgin fore-shadows the even more wonderful conception of her son, and the story of the Redemption begins not with the Annunciation but with the story of Joachim and Anna.

The plays numbered 8 to 11 and play 13, the Visit to Elizabeth, have in common an expositor figure called 'Contemplacio'. There are various indications that these plays were originally a separate series which the compiler of the manuscript was combining with other material. (See Peter Meredith's discussion in Chapter 2.) At the beginning of play 8 the figure of Contemplation addresses the audience and announces the events to be enacted: the conception of Mary, her dedication to the Temple, her marriage, the Annunciation, the meeting with Elizabeth, 'and þer with a conclusion in fewe wordys talked'. After the visit to Elizabeth in play 13 we find the promised conclusion, in which Contemplation thanks the audience for their patience. These two speeches function like a prologue and epilogue, giving to this group of plays the appearance of a self-contained unit. Contemplation's announcement says nothing, however, about Joseph's doubts, the subject of play 12. And there is a further discrepancy between the subjects mentioned in his speech and those mentioned in the procla-mation which appears at the beginning of the manuscript. This proclamation makes no mention of the conception of Mary, her dedication to the Temple, or the visit to Elizabeth, most of the material, that is, which is announced by Contemplation. It seems clear that the compiler was com-bining two separate series of plays, one as announced in the proclamation, the other as announced by Contemplation, and that the joins are still visible. There are, furthermore, marked, even startling, stylistic differ-ences between, on the one hand, the treatment of the conception and dedication of Mary, the Annunciation and the visit to Elizabeth, in plays 8, 9, 11 and 13, and, on the other hand, the treatment of Joseph's doubts in play 12, differences which confirm the impression that what we have to deal with is a combination of plays from two different series. Play 10, the play of the Marriage (a subject mentioned both by the proclamation and by Contemplation), shows signs of being a compound of material from both series.[14]

This diversity of origin explains why the plays in question appear to have different staging requirements.[15] The plays of the Contemplation group (to use a shorthand term for plays 8–11 and 13) seem to have been devised for performance in a single large acting area containing several platforms or structures. Several locations are needed for each play. For example, play 8, on the conception of Mary, needs Joachim and Anna's house in Galilee, the Temple in Jerusalem, Heaven, and Jerusalem's Golden Gate. Play 11 needs Heaven and Joseph and Mary's house. The staging needed for Heaven in this play has to be fairly substantial, for in the scene of the Parliament of Heaven it has to support all three persons of the Trinity, together with angels, archangels and virtues, and the Four Daughters of God, who debate the case for and against Man's redemption. (See Robert Potter's discussion in Chapter 9.) After the debate and the subsequent council of the Trinity, in which the respective claims of justice and mercy are balanced and reconciled, the angel Gabriel is despatched to visit Mary. He must descend in view of the audience; the mediation between heaven and earth is visually represented in the play's staging.

In contrast, plays 12 and 14, the plays of Joseph's doubts and the trial of Joseph and Mary, have more limited staging requirements. It has been suggested that they might have originally been written for the more focused setting of a wagon stage. If so, they could easily have been integrated into the staging of the surrounding plays if they were performed as a sequence. The trial play needs a temple; the play of Joseph's doubts needs a house and heaven, from which God speaks briefly.

The startling effects of contrast produced in this sequence of plays by the juxtaposition of material from different origins presumably did not seem incongruous to the compiler of the manuscript. Perhaps, indeed, the strong tonal contrast appealed to him. The plays of the Contemplation group are characterized by a gravity of treatment and a richness and formality achieved by the use of singing and of citations and paraphrases of the liturgy. There is singing in heaven as the angel descends with his message to Joachim; Mary's ascent of the steps of the temple is accompanied by the recitation of verses from the gradual psalms; during the visit to Elizabeth the Magnificat is recited antiphonally by Mary and Elizabeth, Elizabeth's lines giving an English paraphrase of Mary's Latin verses, both accommodated into a macaronic rhyming stanza. These plays have grandeur and solemnity; they have a cosmic range of reference and also a great intensity of feeling. This range is illustrated in the speech of Contemplation at the beginning of play 11. He speaks here as the representative and spokesman for mankind in an impassioned plea for divine mercy which anticipates the prayers of the angels which follow in the Parliament of Heaven:

> I prey þe lord þi sowlys com se
> How þei ly and sobbe ffor syknes and sorwe

With þi blyssed blood ffrom balys hem borwe   *ransom*
thy careful creaturys cryenge in captyvyte
A tary not gracyous lord tyl it be to-morwe
(19–23).

The speech sets in motion the cosmic action which follows, and establishes a mood of urgency and a sense of involvement which are carried right through to the end of the play, when Gabriel pauses to await Mary's answer, and tells her that the whole universe is also waiting:

Mary come of and haste the
And take hede in thyn entent
Whow þe holy gost · blyssed he be
A-bydeth þin answere and þin assent . . .
Whow all þe blyssyd spyrytes of vertu
þat are in hefne by-ffore goddys face
And all þe gode levers and trew
That Are here in þis erthely place . . .
And þe chosyn sowlys · þis tyme of grace
þat Are in helle and byde rescu . . .
. . . þin Answere desyre to here
and þin Assent to þe incarnacion
(261–80).

There is a sense of awe and also of intense personal involvement in the playing out of the act of divine mercy.

Whereas the play of the Annunciation dramatizes divine revelation, the plays of Joseph's doubts and the trial of Joseph and Mary dramatize human scepticism, first Joseph's scepticism about Mary's virtue and then the scepticism voiced publicly by Mary's detractors. Both Joseph and the detractors are shown to be wrong: human folly is exposed. Appropriately, therefore, the conventions of these two plays are those of satire. In the play of Joseph's doubts the traditions of antimatrimonial satire are even more vigorous than in the equivalent York and Chester plays, as Joseph casts himself in the role of the despised old man whose wanton young wife has taken a young lover.

Alas Alas my name is shent
all men may me now dyspyse
and seyn olde cokwold þi bow is bent
newly now after the frensche gyse
(53–6).

The play of the trial shows the work of a morality dramatist of some accomplishment, a writer with a discriminately distorting eye and a deft hand. Mary and Joseph are haled off to the ecclesiastical court in a motley train of malefactors: Kit Cackler, Lucy Liar, Letice Little-trust, to name only a few. The two detractors, Raise Slander and Backbiter, take a malicious delight in Mary's supposed fall from virtue, and gleefully confront Joseph with what seems to be an irresolvable dilemma: either he must admit to being responsible for Mary's pregnancy, thereby having abetted her in breaking her vow of chastity, or he must admit to being a cuckold. But, as in all good moralities, the Vices play themselves out. When Mary and Joseph each successfully pass through the ordeal of drinking a potion which will disfigure the face of the guilty, Raise Slander accuses the presiding bishop, who is a relative of Mary's, of having fixed the trial, and offers to drink what is left of the potion himself. He immediately falls to the ground complaining of violent pains in the head and begging Mary's pardon for the slander, a comic exemplary moment in the best morality tradition: vice confounded by its own actions. In these two plays, human nature appears at its lowest, and the mode of the plays is appropriately satiric. The clash of mode with the surrounding plays is evidently the result of a compiler's work. He probably found no indecorum in it: it is easy to think of similar violent tonal contrasts within other medieval works.

In the corresponding part of the Towneley cycle the material is more tightly organized and unified in tone. There is, however, a puzzling factor in the Towneley cycle in that it lacks a Nativity play. The Annunciation is preceded by a play of Caesar Augustus which is quite different from the Octavian scenes in the Chester play. Here the Emperor learns of the forthcoming birth of Christ merely as a popular rumour, there is no prophetic sibyl, and he institutes the tax as a means of finding the child. The Emperor here has been modelled on the character of Herod as in the later play of the Magi.

As a whole, the play seems to operate as a contrast to the Annunciation play which follows. Caesar sees the infant Christ merely as an earthly rival; in the following play the true role of Christ in history is explained and recognized. The Annunciation play opens with a prologue spoken by God, recalling the creation of Adam and his fall, and sketching out the parallel patterns of the Fall and the Redemption:

> A man, a madyn, and a tre:
> Man for man, tre for tre,
> Madyn for madyn, thus shal it be.
> (32–4)

There is a contrast, too, within the Annunciation play itself, where the scene of the angel's visit to Mary is paired with the scene of Joseph's doubts. In this pairing of the sacred and the comic the angel's greeting,

> hayll, mary, and well thou be!
> (83).

is echoed in Joseph's words as he enters and starts back, shocked:

> hayll, mary, and well ye be!
> why, bot woman, what chere with the?
> (179–80).

76

The play of the visit to Elizabeth, brief and intimate in tone, is followed immediately by the First Shepherds' Play. There is no representation of the journey to Bethlehem, and the first mention of the birth is when it is announced by the angel to the shepherds. Is there a missing play here? It has been assumed so, and the assumption of loss has been coupled with the suggestion that the cycle as a whole bears signs of incomplete revision.[16] It should be noted, however, that this is not one of the places where the manuscript shows signs of physical loss, and it may also be relevant to note that in the Coventry Shearmen and Tailors' Pageant the material is handled in a way which places the main emphasis on the revelation to the shepherds. Here the play includes the journey to Bethlehem, but there is no focus on the birth itself. Joseph and Mary arrive at the stable and Joseph goes off to fetch help. Then the shepherds appear, call to one another, talk, eat and drink, until they notice the star. The appearance of the star is the only thing that marks the moment of the birth itself, which is thus completely concealed within the shepherd scene. The Coventry play is not, of course, an exact analogy, since it does include the journey to Bethlehem, but it provides a further indication that the events under consideration could be handled in different ways and with different emphases.

The Shearmen and Tailors' Pageant seems to have been typical of the cycle plays at Coventry in grouping several Biblical episodes into a single play. The manuscript of the Towneley cycle, on the other hand, separates the corresponding material into discrete episodes, but it is possible that the method of staging gave a structural framework to these episodes. There are rather fewer clues in the case of Towneley than in the case of the other cycles to the method of staging for which the plays were conceived, but it has been argued, by inference from the action of the plays themselves, that they might be most easily and appropriately accommodated in one fixed locality, with multiple staging, rather than in a processional wagon staging. With this in mind, Martin Stevens, in a discussion of the Towneley Annunciation play,[17] draws attention to the parallel between the prologue of God in this play and that at the beginning of the Creation play, pointing out that these are the only two plays in the cycle to open in this way, and suggesting that the repeated device marks the transition from the era of the Fall to that of the Redemption. The parallel would be pointed by the staging if God spoke both times from the same heaven stage which had been visible throughout.

The York plays, in the confines of their action and their concentration on the figure of the Virgin, form the closest dramatic analogue to the lyric conceit quoted at the beginning of this chapter.[18] But in all of the cycles, in differing ways, a 'lytyl space', in its local particularity and in its symbolic potential, is a vital factor in the dramatization of the two Biblical events of the Annunciation and the Nativity.

77

Producing Miracles

Darryll Grantley

One of the thornier problems associated with the study of early theatre production is how miracles were originally staged. They often require very sophisticated and varied technical effects but usually very little indication is given as to how these effects were achieved. It is perfectly possible for readers to go through these plays without realizing how sophisticated the technical aspects of their production need to be. Miracles and stage effects occur in all the varieties of medieval dramatic production but, because of the importance of the miracle in the saints' plays, they are one of the more challenging areas of study from the point of view of stage production. Saints' or conversion plays draw upon the large body of legendary hagiographic writings for their material. In these legends the occurrence of miracles is of enormous significance. They frequently constitute the climax of a saint's legend and are, at the very least, an essential part of it.

The function of miracles in saints' legends can be seen broadly as twofold. One is to prove the holiness and power of the saint. Miracles frequently commence soon after the saint's renunciation of the world.[1] Such miracles usually take the form of the deliverance of the saint from tortures, a manifestation of healing or other beneficial powers by the saint or his or her defeat of heathen gods, idols or other malevolent powers with divine help. Often the burial place of the saint also acquired miraculous properties. These miracles were often used to serve the second purpose too: that of a testament to the power of God which results directly in the conversion of sinners. This is sometimes what prompts the saint's conversion in the legends but more usually the miracle is worked by the saint and onlookers are persuaded by it to accept the faith.

A recent definition of the saint's play stresses the element of miracle:

> A saint's play is a play that has a saint as its protagonist or a miracle as its main action.[2]

The extant English plays which fall into this category are few in number, having been an obvious target for suppression during the Reformation.

78

They are widely different in character, which suggests that the saint's play could take several forms, and it is doubtful whether their writers would have recognized them as belonging to a specific type of play at all. The four plays which fall into this broad definition of saints', miracle or conversion plays are the Digby manuscript plays of *Mary Magdalen* and *The Conversion of St. Paul*, the Croxton *Play of the Sacrament* and the Cornish *Meriasek*. Since the Croxton play does not deal with the life of a saint at all and *Meriasek* does not involve the conversion of its central character, perhaps the only thing these plays have in common is a strong and decisive element of miracle.

The forms and functions of miracles in these plays include those cited above. *Mary Magdalen*, for instance, has the saint destroying the heathen temple by means of divine visitation and later appearing to the pagan king and queen in a dream, actions which culminate in the conversion of the couple. In the same play two resurrections are shown apart from that of Christ, both effected through the agency of the saint. In *The Conversion of St. Paul* and the Croxton play the manifestation of divine power results in the conversion of the central characters and in *Meriasek* the several miracles which pervade the play usually demonstrate the healing power of the saint and what generally follows is a conversion to or an affirmation of Christian faith.

Many of the miracles in these plays do not require the use of devices or elaborate stage effects. Such are the resurrections of Lazarus and the queen of Marcyll in *Mary Magdalen*, the restoration of Saul's sight in *The Conversion of St. Paul* and the frequent occurrences of the healing of the sick, lame and blind in *Meriasek*. Skilful acting alone is sufficient to bring out the dramatic impact of these. However, stage devices did play an important part in producing miraculous effects in medieval drama. That these were often highly sophisticated and ingenious should not be doubted. An account of 1392 by Richard Maydiston of a pageant device for ascents and descents from a tower without visible aids shows both the pleasure which these devices could give to an audience:

> Cerneret has facies quisquis, puto, non dubitaret
> Nil fore sub coelo quod sibi plus placeat

> (Whoever saw these [suspended] figures I think, could doubt that anything under heaven would please him more)

> (Quoted in Wickham, p. 69)

and their effectiveness in concealing their workings:

> Nubibus inclusi veniunt, et in aethere pendunt,
> Quo tamen ingenio nescio, crede mihi
> (They came surrounded by clouds and hung in the air, by what device I know not, believe me)

> (Quoted in Wickham, p. 70)

An account of the Passion play at Valenciennes in 1547 indicates the wonder which the stage devices excited in a fairly sophisticated audience:

> Aux festes de Pentecoste de l'an 1547, les principaux bourgeois de la ville réprésentèrent sur le théâtre en la maison du duc d'Arschot la vie, mort et passion de Notre Seigneur en vingt-cinq journées, en chacune desquelles on vit paraître des choses estranges et pleines d'admiration. Les secrets du Paradis et de l'Enfer estoient tout à fait prodigieux, et capables d'estre pris par la populace pour enchantements. Car l'on voyait la Verite, les Anges et divers personnages descendre de bien haut, tantost visiblement, autrefois comme invisibles, puis paroistre tout à coup.
> (During the feast of Pentecost in 1547 the leading citizens of the town staged, in the theatre at the home of the duc d'Arschot, the life, death and Passion of Our Lord in twenty five days, on each of which were seen things both strange and full of wonder. The devices of Heaven and Hell were amazing and able to be regarded by the people as magic. For one saw Truth, the Angels and various characters descend from a fair height, sometimes visibly, sometimes invisibly, to make a sudden appearance.)[3]

It is easy to see, therefore, how effective stage tricks could be in representing miracles. Since they themselves appeared to be miraculous, they contributed to the credibility of the wonders being presented on stage.

The producers of medieval plays were fully aware of the importance of good devices to stage miraculous effects. French records show that skilful masters of such devices were in great demand (see Cohen, pp. 143–4) and it is likely that the same would have been the case in England with her wealthy guilds and areas of strong dramatic tradition. Because of the dearth of detail about stage devices in those English dramatic records that remain extant, it is useful to draw to a large extent on Continental and specifically French sources where such details are often fuller, but the frequency of directions in English plays calling for mechanical stage effects and the evidence from such records as do exist indicate that stagecraft in England was quite up to producing a variety of stage miracles.

Perhaps the easiest to manage of all the miraculous effects in the four plays under discussion is the expulsion of the seven devils from the body of Mary in *Mary Magdalen*, a miracle mentioned in Mark xvi . 9 and Luke viii . 2. In the play the stage direction is as follows:

> *Wyth þis word seuyn dyllys xall dewoyde from*   issue
> *þe woman, and the Bad Angyll entyr into hell with thondyr.*
> (691 sd.)

It is possible that Mary wore a voluminous cloak from which issued the seven devils, which may have been played by small boys. In *Wisdom* the devils run out from under the cloak of the Soul:

> *Here rennyt owt from wndyr þe horrybyll mantyll of þe Soull seven small boys in þe lyknes of dewyllys and so retorne ageyn.*
> (912 sd.)

However, another possibility is that Mary stood in front of a screen behind which stood the devils who then ran out between her legs. This appears to have been the way a similar miracle was staged in the Bourges *Mystère des Actes des Apôtres* of 1536 where Christ cast a devil out of St. Denis:

> *Jesus-Crist descende du paradis et vient à la prison où est saint Denys pour luy communier. Doit sortir ung diable dentre les jambes de la.*
>
> (Jesus Christ descends from heaven (stage) and comes to the prison in which St. Denis is lodged in order to administer communion to him. A devil must come out from between the legs of that man.)
>
> (Girardot, p. 27)

The miracle in *Mary Magdalen* takes place in the house of Simon the Leper and it is possible that the scaffold which represented it had a front stage on which the action could take place and a curtained off rear section.[4] Mary would stand in front of this curtain and the devils could then emerge from the rear chamber where they were concealed. Accompanied by loud noise ('thondyr') and possibly smoke as was customary with the appearance of devils, the dramatic impact of this miracle would have been considerable.

Other miracles which probably involved special design and construction of the scaffolds in which they took place, also in *Mary Magdalen*, are the quaking of the idols in 1553 sd. and the 'sinking' of the heathen priest and boy in 1561 sd. These are important miracles because, along with the firing of the temple which occurs a little later in the play, they represent the victory of the saint over the forces of paganism. The quaking of the idol was probably done manually by someone concealed in the scaffold as was the case in a production of the Mons *Mystère de la Passion* in 1501. In the staging manual there is an instruction that the person who is to topple the idols is to be warned to be ready:

> *Soit cy adverti de faire trebuchier les ydoles du temple quant on le dira.*
>
> (This man should be warned to topple the idols of the temple when he is told.)[5]

and a few lines further on the direction is given for the idols to be toppled. The idol in *Mary Magdalen* would probably have stood on a pedestal or perhaps the altar itself and could easily have been shaken from underneath by someone concealed behind the altar or under the floor of the scaffold, though in a modern production of the play by the University of Durham in 1982 a thin cord passed from the top of the idol through the back wall of the temple so that it could be shaken from behind and the cord also prevented it from being toppled completely. It is probable, however, that the scaffold would have had a raised floor under which people could have been concealed. This construction could be used too to execute the direction that the priest and the boy should 'synke'. A trapdoor behind or even in front of the altar could quickly drop the two out of sight into the space below. A small trench might have been dug by which they made their way out. In the *Résurrection* attributed to Jean Michel, a trapdoor and underground passages were used:

> *Et Jésus, vestu de blanc, accompaigné de troys anges, Michel, Raphaël et Uriel, doit soudainement et subtilement saillir de dessoubs terre de coste son tombeau, par une petite trappe de boys, couverte de terre, laquelle se reclost sans qu'on s'en apperçoive.*
> (And Jesus, dressed in white, accompanied by three angels, Michael, Raphael and Uriel, should suddenly and secretly emerge from under the ground at the side of his tomb by a little wooden trapdoor covered with earth, which should shut again without being noticed.)
>
> (Quoted in Cohen, p. 162)

The disappearance of the priest and boy takes place simultaneously with the firing of the temple and the sudden distraction of the audience's attention caused by that spectacle would allow the trapdoor to open and shut again without being noticed.

Other miracles which involve elaborate scaffold devices are the opening of heaven to reveal the risen Christ, the ascents and descents of the angels and the elevation of Mary, all in *Mary Magdalen*. After his Ascension, Christ appears in heaven, the stage direction being:

> *Her xall hevyn opyn, and Jhesus xall shew [hymself]*
> (1348 sd.).

The heaven stage would, mechanically at least, have been the most elaborate of all the scaffolds. Christ would have been standing on the upper platform of this tall structure, tall and dominating enough to show Heaven's ascendancy over Hell (itself quite high, having an upper platform set over a Hell-mouth). The heaven stage would have to have been of a substantial size so that it could accommodate not only Christ himself but at least one angel and possibly a choir as suggested by the stage directions after lines 2030 and 2122 which both require there to be rejoicing in the heavens. The 'opening' of heaven could have been effected simply by the drawing back of a curtain but a more probable and dramatic effect is suggested by the Cornish *Creacion of the World* where the opening direction is:

> *The Father must be in a clowde and when he speakethe of Heaven let the levys open.*

It is not stated exactly what is meant by this but, rather than a simple hinged arrangement like a door, it is most probable that the covering screen consisted of panels in the shape of clouds which pulled apart when activated by a pulley mechanism. It is possible too that the 'levys' or folds of cloud were attached to a fan mechanism so that they slid apart by folding into one another. Both these methods could be used to keep Christ's lower half obscured to give the impression of his rising out of the clouds as suggested by numerous contemporary illustrations and also by the direction in the Chester cycle where Christ is directed to stand *in medio quasi supra nubes* (in the middle, half above the clouds, *Chester*, p. 373).[6]

Ascents and descents to and from the upper platform of the heaven stage were not an uncommon feature of medieval plays and pageants. Modern productions have tended to use concealed staircases or ladders as in a production of *Mary Magdalen* at the University of Colorado in Boulder in 1976 and also the Durham production. However, in the early theatre these ascents and descents were very much part of the visible miraculous effect and, where possible, were managed by means of ropes, pulleys and windlasses.[7] The use of clouds to conceal the mechanism can be seen in a complicated direction for the Ascension of Christ in the *Résurrection* attributed to Jean Michel:

> *Doit estre avec lui [Christ], Gabriel, Raphaël, Carinus, Leoncius et le doit on veoir les jambes par-dessoulz l'engin et par dessus le chief et les mains joincts . . . et les cordes qui tireront l'instrument ou Jhésus sera doivent estre mussées de toile en maniere de nue.*
> (With him [Christ] there must be Gabriel, Raphael, Carinus, Leoncius and their legs must be seen below the device and the head above and hands joined . . . and the ropes carrying the instrument on which Jesus will be transported must be concealed with fabric in the form of clouds.)
>
> (Quoted in Cohen, p. 154)

Mary Magdalen requires the ascent and descent of several people at once, especially when the angels raise Mary into the clouds to feed her with manna. It is likely that some sort of lift platform was used, perhaps covered in fabric to represent cloud. Christ's instruction in l. 2006 is:

> Angellys! Into þe clowdys ye do hyr havns.   ᵡ *raise up*

and another descending cloud is used to effect a divine miracle earlier in the play when the temple is set on fire.

Another miracle requiring mechanical contrivance is the bleeding of the Host in the Croxton play. A contemporary account of a 1513 French play of the Sacrament of Metz suggests that there blood was an important part of the effect:

> *Alors par ung secret, qui estoit fait, sorti grand abondance de sang et sailloit en hault parmi ladite hostie, comme si ce fut ung enfant qui pissoit, et en fut le juif tout guste et dessaigné et faisoit moult bien son personnaige.*
> (Then by a device which had been made, a large quantity of blood sprang up high from the said Host, as if it was a pissing infant and the Jew was covered and bloodied by it and it made his person very wet.)[8]

It has sometimes been suggested that the dramatic use of blood in the Croxton play is a sensationalistic element but it is wholly in keeping with the bloody traditions of the saint's legend where detailed accounts of gruesome punishments are legion. In the play there are two directions for the use of blood:

> *Here þe Ost must blede* (480 sd.)

and

> *Here þe owyn must ryve asunder and blede owt at þe cranys, and an image appere owt with woundys bledyng.* (712 sd.)

It is likely that real animal blood or a blood coloured liquid was used as in the Lucerne Passion play. Compare the following directions from that play:

> *Cayn sol haben ein Howen, die allso gerüst, das zuo vorderst ein höle, darinn bluott oder bluot farb sye*
> (Cain should have an hoe which at the very tip should have a hole in which there is blood colouring.)

and:

> *Longinus hatt ein spär darnach gerüst zum stechen in Saluatoris brust, ist Hol vnd glych einer sprützen, sol vornen bluot farb im ysen beschlossen haben.*
> (Longinus has a spear poised to stab into the Saviour's breast; it is hollow and like a syringe and the tip should have a blood colouring contained in the iron.)[9]

For the bleeding of the Host in the Croxton play it is possible that blood filled bellows may have been used to create a fountain of blood. This was the method employed in a modern production in 1977 by the Medieval Players. A rubber air mattress pump was used. However, a tightly filled bladder inside the sacramental loaf would have much the same effect. The dialogue and directions of the play suggest that such a bladder was concealed right in the middle of the loaf. The four Jews first stab the four sides of the loaf:

> *Here shall the iiij Jewys pryk þer daggerys in iiij quarters* (468 sd.)

but it is only when Jonathas·runs his dagger right through it with the words:

> A stowte stroke also for to stryke
> In the myddys yt shalbe sene! (479–80)

that the Host begins to bleed.

The second instance of miraculous bleeding on stage also involves the splitting apart of the oven. Here one may conjecture an oven which consisted of two halves hinged at the bottom so that, at the operation of a mechanism to release the two halves, perhaps by explosive means or in conjunction with an explosive effect, they would fall apart giving the impression of the oven's having split down the middle. Blood could then pour out of holes in the side of the oven.

The 'image' of the bleeding Christ is required to appear out of the oven

84

in 712 sd. A modern production of the play by the Medieval Players used an actor for this (see Plate 6) but the word 'image' suggests that a picture or small model would have been used in original productions. In 825 sd. it has to change back into a loaf on stage. This could have been managed by a lowering of the 'image' out of sight, the Host then rising into view in its place, but early stagecraft was quite equal to managing the spectacle of the metamorphosis in full view of the audience. In the French play of the miracle of the Host this was apparently done on stage:

> *Et alors comme enragie (il?) print l'hostie et la ruoit en un chaudière d'yoaue*
> *boullant et elle se elevoit en l'air et montoit en une nuée et devint un petit enfant*
> *en montant a mont et se faisoit tout ceci par engins et secrets.*
> (And then as if mad (he) took the Host and cast it in a cauldron of boiling water
> and it rose in the air and rose on a cloud and became a small infant while rising
> and all these things were done by engines and devices)[10]

The nature of these devices is not explained but the answer lies perhaps in the clockwork machinery which was used in pageant theatre. The complexity and sophistication of this machinery can be seen from the following account of a pageant to celebrate a visit of the Emperor Charles V to London in 1522:

> Also ther were ij goodly ymages one in a castell lyke to the
> emprowr in visage, and the other in an herbar wyth rosys   *arbour*
> lyke to the kynges grace with ij swerdys nakyd in ther
> handys. Which castell, garden and the ymages dyd Ryse by a
> Vyce. The ymages dyd beholde eche other, and then cast   *device*
> away ther swerdys by a vyce, and wt another vyce ioyned
> eche to other and embrasede eche other in tokennyng off
> love and pease, whiche don an ymage off the father off
> hevyn all burnyd golde dyd disclose and appare and move in
> the topp of the pageant.
>
> (Quoted in Wickham, p. 84)

In the Croxton play, miraculous dramatic effect is of particular importance since the focus of the play is on the miracles surrounding the Host rather than on any saintly character.

Another important effect in this play is the boiling of the cauldron, the water in it turning to blood, as directed in 672 sd. It is possible that a churn within the cauldron was operated to stir up the water, but the water was required to boil over as indicated by Malchas' words:

> All thys oyle waxyth redde as blood,
> And owt of the cawdron yt begynnyth to rin.
> (674–5)

The most likely solution is the use of a fountain, the outlet of which would have been concealed just under the surface of the liquid to give the impression of boiling when it spurted. It would also have brought about the

Plate 6: *The miraculous appearance of the image of Christ from the oven, from the 1981 production of* The Croxton Play *by the Medieval Players.*

overflow of the liquid from the cauldron and, if the incoming liquid contained red dye, give the impression that the liquid in the cauldron was turning to blood. Fountains were not an uncommon feature of medieval dramatic presentations (see Wickham, pp. 90–1, 225, 244 and 399) and if the cauldron were placed on the ground it would not have been difficult to supply it with a conduit.

A miracle involving water is to be found also in *Meriasek*. After a prayer by the saint in lines 667–71 the direction appears:

her ye wyll sprynggyth vp water

This miracle clearly takes place in the open space away from any scaffold as he is directed to go across to a meadow just before his prayer. This again could have been staged by means of an underground conduit either activated by someone offstage or with a stopper at the fountainhead which could be surreptitiously broken or removed by the actor playing Meriasek. The Cornish *Origo Mundi* has a similar effect, when Moses causes water to flow from a rock on striking it. (See Norris, Vol. I, p. 140.) It is possible that both plays were taking advantage of the possibilities offered by the same location.

The most spectacular dramatic effects, however, and those perhaps most suitable for the portrayal of miracles are those involving fire and light. The medieval stage commonly employed a range of pyrotechnic effects frequently, but by no means always, associated with devils and 'diableries'. The English saints' plays use fire and light on several occasions in their staging of miraculous events. A striking instance of this is to be found in *The Conversion of St. Paul* where the central miracle which brings about the conversion is a flash of lightning which throws Saul off his horse. The direction in the play is:

Here comyth a feruent, wyth gret tempest, and Saule faulyth down of hys horse
(182 sd.)

'Feruent' is best taken to mean 'a flash' and it dramatizes the *lux de coelo* of Acts ix . 3. In outdoor productions the creation of flashes of light would have presented a problem to medieval producers, though medieval plays abound in directions for sudden illuminations. Candles and lamps would clearly not have had the desired effect. In a 15th century play of the conversion of St. Paul, there is the direction:

Lors sy comme Saulus passera par dessoulz Paradis, Jhesus prengne .l. brandon ardant, et gete sus ly, et lors il se lesse cheoir a terre.
(Then as Saul passes below Heaven, Jesus takes the burning torch and throws (it) on him and then he falls to the ground)[11]

However, the direction in the English play does not suggest that a similar method was employed there. What may have been used are explosive fireworks which appear to have been used elsewhere in the play at the entry of the devils (Cf. 411 sd. and 432 sd.). In the same play there is the direction:

> *Hic aparebit Spiritus Sanctus super eum* (291 sd.)
> (Here the Holy Spirit shall appear above him).

This apparently simple stage direction may also suggest a fire effect since the descent of the Holy Spirit was often represented in medieval drama by means of fire. In *Chester* Play XXI, for instance, there is the direction:

> *Tunc Deus emittet Spiritum Sanctum in spetie ignis* (238 sd.)
> (Then God sends the Holy Spirit in the form of fire).

However, perhaps the most interesting direction for this type of representation of the Holy Spirit occurs in the *Résurrection* attributed to Jean Michel. Here the Spirit descends upon the Virgin and apostles, seated in a cenacle:

> *Icy endroit doit descendre grant brandon de feu artificiellement fait par eaue de vie et doit visiblement descendre en la maison du cénacle sur notre dame et sur les femmes et apostres, qui doivent être assis . . . sur chascun d'eulx doit choir une langue de feu ardent du dit brandon et seront vingt et un en nombre.*
> (In this place a great torch of fire artificially made with eau de vie should descend, and descend visibly in the scaffold of the cenacle upon Our Lady and upon the women and the apostles, who should be seated . . . on each one of them a tongue of burning flame from the said torch should fall and there must be twenty one in number.) (Quoted in Cohen, p. 156)

The descent of the Spirit in the Digby play is unlikely to have been as elaborate as this but, in a play which does make some use of light and fire effects, some sort of pyrotechnic device would possibly have been used to represent it.

In *Meriasek* there are several different instances of light and fire to suggest miracles. The first comes in 1835 sd.:

> *Cum in aquam descendisset baptismatis mirabilis enituit splendor lucis Sic inde mundus exiuit et christum se vidisse asseruit.*
> (When he went down into the water of baptism there shone forth a marvellous splendour of light. So thence he came forth clean, and declared he had seen Christ.)

There should be some reservation about accepting this as a stage direction, however. It is longer than others in the play and it is in the past tense whereas the other directions are in the imperative or indicative present. The writer may be quoting directly from a legendary source. However, that an attempt would have been made in the staging of the play to represent this light is indicated by Constantine's comment in lines 1844–5 on the light that had shone a few moments previously. A light may also have shone from the face of Constantine and it is possible that his face was covered with a reflective substance which gave it a resplendent quality. The possibility of this is suggested by the fact that the direction quoted above occurs directly after a separate direction for his mask to be removed (*ye vysour away*). Various French plays contain directions for such make up to suggest radiance, e.g. the Greban *Passion*:

> *Icy doivent les habiz de Jhesus blans et sa face resplendissante comme d'or.*
> (Here the clothing of Jesus must be white and his face shining like gold.)[12]

and the Mons *Passion* of 1501 contains the following direction:

> *Nota que icy Jhesus entre dedens la montaigne pour soy vestir d'une robe blance et la plus blance que trouver se p[o]uelt, et une face at les mains d'or bruni.*
> (Note that here Jesus enters into the mountain to vest himself in a white robe and the whitest that can be found, with a face and hands of burnished gold.)[13]
> gold.)[13]

Since this make up was most often used to represent transfiguration, it would have been an appropriate method of dramatizing Constantine's new-found state of grace.

One of the pyrotechnic effects in *Meriasek* involves a fiery dragon, clearly of some size since some of the soldiers are swallowed by it in 3949 sd. The miracle consists of St. Silvester's taming of it. This type of miracle, the taming or putting to flight of wild beasts by a saint, is fairly common in the legends and in the *Legenda Aurea* is to be found, for instance, in the legends of St. Hilary, St. Anthony, St. George, St. Peter, St. Martha, St. Donatus and St. Matthew the Apostle as well as that of St. Silvester. The effectiveness of the miracle in this play as stage business is enhanced by the fire which issues from its mouth, very probably managed by igniting pipes containing gunpowder or some other flammable substance, as suggested by the direction:

> *her a gonn yn y dragon ys movthe aredy & fyr*   (3946 sd.)

The construction of the dragon itself would seem to have been quite elaborate; it may have been mounted on wheels and had a hinged mouth to open and close. It invites comparison with the dragon in the Bourges *Mystère des Actes des Apôtres*:

> *Marchoit après un grant dragon de longeur environ de douze pieds, mouvant sans cesse la teste, les yeux, la queue, et tirant la langue d'où issoit du feu assez souvent.*
> (A big dragon came next of about twelve feet in length, ceaselessly moving its head, eyes, tail and putting out its tongue from which issued fire very frequently.)
> (Girardot, p. 6)

The dragon in *Meriasek* is used for a single, relatively minor miracle and then is not seen again. This fact gives some idea of the technical elaborateness of the staging of the play and the lengths to which producers were prepared to go to achieve spectacular effects. This effect was probably added later as directions for it are in English in a later hand, whereas the other stage directions in the play are in Latin.

Perhaps the most elaborate and spectacular of the pyrotechnic tricks used to portray miracles in the plays under discussion is, however, the firing of the temple in *Mary Magdalen*. After a prayer from the saint the heathen temple of Marcyll (Marseilles) is miraculously set alight. The direction is straightforward but specific:

> *Here xall comme a clowd from heven, and sett þe tempyl on afyer, and þe pryst and þe cler[k] xall synke . . .*
>
> (1561 sd.)

This type of miracle, involving either the contest of strengths between the Christian and heathen gods, or destruction of pagan gods by a saint is one commonly found in legend. In the *Legenda Aurea* it is to be found in some form in the legends of St. Thomas the Apostle, St. Urban, St. Vitus, St. Stephen the Pope and St. Callixtus. In the play the miracle has great thematic significance as it represents the victory of the saint over the forces of paganism and its presentation on stage would have been as dramatic and realistic as possible. The descent of the cloud from heaven would most probably have been managed by means of pulleys and ropes. The scaffold representing the heathen temple would obviously have been positioned close to the heaven stage, which would have been a rather high structure for the reasons already discussed. A similar descent of a cloud from heaven to a specific location was also required in the Bourges *Actes des Apôtres*:

> *Fault qu'il soit envoyé de Paradis jusques sur led. monument une nue ronde en forme de couronne où aye plusieurs anges faincts tenans en leurs mains espées nues et dards.*
> (There must be sent from Heaven to the said monument a round cloud in the form of a crown, on which there must be several artificial angels holding in their hands bare swords and spears.)
>
> (Girardot, p. 15)

Whether the cloud was actually instrumental in igniting the temple in *Mary Magdalen* or whether it was ignited simultaneously with the impact of the cloud, it is difficult to say. For the play of *Old Tobit* the inventory of properties lists:

> a firmament, with a fiery cloud and a double cloud
>
> (Wickham, p. 246)

It is doubtful that this cloud was used with actual fire but it does suggest that the concept of fiery clouds was in dramatic use. The temple itself would probably have had a channel of aqua vitae soaked oakum across the front which may have been ignited by a lighted firebrand attached to the cloud. A device recorded by Bishop Abraham of Souzdal in 1439 accomplished the simultaneous lighting of all the lamps of a church by fire which descended from above in the course of an Annunciation play. (See Tydeman, p. 174.) The direction in *Mary Magdalen* may be suggesting something similar but it is equally possible that the substance in the temple could have been secretly set on fire by a stagehand on the impact of the cloud. Whatever the case, the dramatic impact would have been great. As with many stage miracles, the spectacle is used here to reinforce the theme of divine power in the play and it does so in the most dramatic way possible.

Even such a cursory examination as this of stage miracles and their production in the saints' plays shows that there are many unsolved problems with regard to medieval stagecraft and also that it made use of a range of sophisticated technical devices to a far greater extent than is generally supposed. The necessity for miraculous effect and trompe l'oeil in miracles frequently made great demands on the ingenuity of medieval producers, an ingenuity which is unfortunately too little recorded, especially in England, and which has often to be reconstructed by analogy and conjecture. However, sketchy as our knowledge may be, cognizance has to be taken of the stage production of miracles for a full appreciation especially of saints' plays since in these it constitutes a most important part of their visual impact. Miracles, an essential element in the dramatic action of saints' plays, are often too easily passed over on the page where directions are frequently brief and undramatic.

The Virtue of Perseverance

Richard Proudfoot

Morality plays have invented actions – unlike biblical plays, liturgical or other, whose subject is universal human history, seen in terms of divine purpose and divine intervention in it, – even though they may be (and usually are) composed of traditional materials and share a common concern with the destiny and destination of a single but representative human soul. If biblical plays are histories, moralities are homilies. Their actions are allegorical, as are their dramatis personae, and they vary in scope, length and outcome.

Five or six English religious moralities survive from the fifteenth and early sixteenth centuries. Others must once have existed, though probably not in such large numbers as biblical plays or plays on the lives of saints. Lost plays which were presumably allegorical include the York plays of *The Creed* and *Pater Noster*, and *Pater Noster* plays recorded at Beverley and Lincoln. *Pater Noster* plays probably related the seven petitions of the Lord's prayer to the seven Works of Mercy.

The earliest surviving English morality, *The Pride of Life* (? c. 1400), is fragmentary, breaking off after 502 lines (about half an hour's playing time). Its protagonist, Rex Vivus, abetted by Strength and Health, plans to live for ever and rudely rejects his Queen's pleas that he should think of the church. She summons Bishop, who warns the king to think of his ending. King Life is rude to Bishop and instead sends his messenger, Mirth or Solas, to challenge Death. What was to ensue is revealed by the Prologue: Death accepts the challenge and proceeds to slay the king, his family and his knights.

> Qwhen þe body is doun ibroȝt
>   Þe soule sorow awakith;
> Þe bodyis pride is dere aboȝt   ˈ--ʊ *dearly bought*
>   Þe soule þe fendis takith.
>   (93–6)

The release of the soul was then to be obtained by the 'priere of Oure Lady mylde' to 'her son so mylde' (96–9).

92

Everyman, translated from a Dutch morality printed in 1518, and itself printed in four editions between about 1520 and 1530, tells the same story, but in very different terms. Everyman is no king: the images are mercantile. Unexpectedly summoned by Death, Everyman is granted a brief respite to seek company on his coming journey and to set his account-book in order. Company on the journey of death is not forthcoming, except for that of his Good Deeds (the English author's anti-Reformation substitute for the Faith of the original). Confession and Penitence prepare Everyman to die. He does so in a new costume, signifying penitence, in the correct frame of mind and spirit, and with the appropriate quotation from Luke xxiii.46.

> In to thy handes, Lorde, my soule I commende;
> Receyue it, Lorde, that it be not lost.
> As thou me boughtest, so me defende,
> And saue me from the fendes boost,
> That I may appere with that blessyd hoost
> That shall be saued at the day of dome.
> *In manus tuas*, of myghtes moost
> For euer, *Commendo spiritum meum.*
>
> (880–7)

Such echoing of Christ's words from the cross was widely recommended to the dying. Popular belief accepted the saying of '*in manus tuas*' before death as a prophylactic against the snares of the devil, though preachers, while not rejecting it outright, advised against sole reliance on so easy a course. That the formula also attracted some scepticism may be seen in the parody introduced by the Wakefield author of the Second Shepherds' Play. Mak, the thief, prepares for sleep with the words '*manus tuas commendo/ poncio pilato*'. Everyman's journey never takes place: the body merely sinks into its grave, in a strikingly theatrical translation of the metaphoric vehicle 'journey' into its tenor, 'death' – though a final comment assures us of the soul's salvation.

Mankind and *Wisdom* or *Mind, Will and Understanding*, both probably plays of the 1460s and preserved in the same fifteenth-century manuscript, vary the action by stopping short of death. They present a different pattern, in which the central character undergoes initial temptation followed by a return to the fold and eventual cleansing. The protagonist of *Mankind* is caught between the exhortations of Mercy and the distracting temptations of Mischief, Nought, New-Guise and Nowadays. The action hinges on the sins of idleness and careless talk and reaches its major climax in a star appearance by a devil, Titivillus. Mankind is distracted from work and prayer, has his coat, signifying his state of moral health, removed and cut short and is reduced to despair and to the contemplation of suicide. Mercy returns to admonish and restore him in an explicitly moralizing ending, which includes the instruction 'Synne not in hope of mercy' (845).

Wisdom is as spiritual and theological in emphasis and language as *Mankind*, for all the seriousness of its argument, is physical and scatological. Its central character, though not its most prominent role, is Anima, the soul, torn, this time, between the counsels of Wisdom, who is Christ, and Lucifer. Costume is elaborately prescribed and is clearly intended to bear considerable weight of significance, as Meg Twycross has shown above. Wisdom embodies royalty, 'in a ryche purpull clothe of golde wyth a mantyll of the same ermynnyde wythin, hawynge abowt hys neke a ryall hood furred wyth ermyn, wpon hys hede a cheweler [*chevelure* = wig] wyth browys, a berde of golde of sypres curlyed, a ryche imperyall crown þerwpon sett wyth precyus stonys and perlys, in hys leyftehonde a balle of golde wyth a cros þerwppon and in hys ryght honde a regall schepter' (*Macro*, p. 114). The contrasting vice is Lucifer, 'in a dewyllys aray wythowt and wythin as a prowde galonte' (325 sd.), personifying the worldliness which is the soul's chief temptation.

Lucifer's tempting speeches are addressed to the soul's three 'mights' or faculties, Mind, Will and Understanding. He persuades them to reject the contemplative life for active life in the world, citing the example of Christ's own ministry and hypocritically urging that 'Gode lowyt a clene sowll and a mery' (494). Costume changes transform Mind into Pride, Will into Lust and Understanding into Avarice (sins associated, respectively, with the Devil, the Flesh and the World). After revelry, which includes an emblematic dance by the followers of each in turn, they fall to quarrelling, until Wisdom returns and brings them to repentance. Anima had started in a costume of black and white:

Blake by sterynge of synne þat cummyth all-day,	*incitement*
Wyche felynge cummythe of sensualyte,	
Ande wyght by knowenge of reson veray	*white*
Off þe blyssyde infenyt Deyte.	

(153–6)

After the defection of her 'mights', she changes – 'Here ANIMA apperythe in þe most horrybull wyse, fowlere þan a fende' (902 sd.) – but when penitence cleanses her – 'Here rennyt owt from wndyr þe horrybyll mantyll of þe SOULL seven small boys in þe lyknes of dewyllys' (912 sd.). For the final scene, the soul and the mights resume their first costumes, 'all hauyng on crownys, syngynge in here commynge in: *Quid retribuam Domino pro omnibus que retribuit mihi?*' (1064 sd.).

The Castle of Perseverance is both the earliest complete English morality and the most ambitious and comprehensive. It dates from the first quarter of the fifteenth century and may have originated in the Lincoln area, though the only extant manuscript was apparently copied by a Norfolk scribe about 1440. This manuscript was in the collection of the Rev. Cox Macro of Bury St. Edmund's in the early eighteenth century, together with *Mankind* and

Wisdom. In 1819, the three plays, which have come to be known as the 'Macro Plays', were bound into a single volume (since 1936 in the Folger Shakespeare Library, Washington, D.C.).

Almost all of the themes and techniques in the other English moralities are incorporated in the *Castle*, together with many more. These include: regal and military imagery; structural use of metaphors, especially that of life as a journey; scenes of temptation and penitential recovery; the issue of death-bed repentance and its debatable validity; significant costumes and costume changes; and the use at moments of climax of vocal music.

Everyman has conventionally been regarded as the great English morality, though this estimate was shaken by the demonstration that it is a translation. The judgement had its origins in the eighteenth century, when the *Castle* (first printed in its entirety as late as 1904) was still unknown, and it was easily sustained by later generations to whom *Everyman* recommended itself by its simplicity and its modest staging demands – not to mention its profusion of parts for women. In our own time, the increasing frequency of productions of the *Castle* has done much to redress the balance.

Thomas Percy, in an essay 'On the Origin of the English Stage' published in his *Reliques of Ancient English Poetry* (1765), wrote of *Everyman* in these terms.

> *Every Man* is a grave solemn piece, not without some rude attempts to excite terror and pity, and therefore may not improperly be referred to the class of Tragedy. It is remarkable that in this old simple drama the fable is conducted upon the strictest model of the Greek Tragedy. The action is simply one, the time of action is that of the performance, the scene is never changed, nor the stage ever empty. Every-man, the hero of the piece, after his first appearance never withdraws, except when he goes out to receive the sacraments, which could not well be exhibited in public; and during his absence Knowledge descants on the excellence and power of the priesthood, somewhat after the manner of the Greek chorus. And indeed, except in the circumstance of Every-man's expiring on the stage, the Sampson Agonistes of Milton is hardly formed on a severer plan.[1]

Such a critique exhibits several unhelpful prejudices, among them the assumed universal applicability of Aristotelian, or more strictly, neo-classical, criteria of dramatic structure and the fallacious supposition that early = primitive. What is most strikingly absent is any knowledge of the ends or means of late medieval drama, such as acquaintance with the *Castle* might either have supplied or at least identified as desirable. No play less like a Greek tragedy in form and technique than the *Castle* could easily be imagined: yet it clearly represents the peak of a very different kind of highly developed dramatic art.

The Castle of Perseverance is – or rather was before it lost two leaves, containing some 200 lines of verse – about 3850 lines long (comparable with the uncut text of Shakespeare's *Richard III* or even *Hamlet*), but its action can be briefly outlined without substantial distortion.

> The play opens with the World, the Devil, and the Flesh on their thrones, the three kings who boast of their purpose to destroy Mankind. He appears on the ground below as a new-born child, naked and feeble, and is soon persuaded by his Bad Angel to go to the World and become rich and lordlike. Clothed in fine array by Pleasure and given gold and silver by Sir Covetousness, he hugs all the sins to his bosom. When his Good Angel calls for help, Penance pierces Mankind with a lance and Shrift gives him confession and absolution. The Virtues guard him in their castle against the assaults of the Devil and the Flesh. Covetousness, however, tempts Mankind in old age to forsake his hope of heaven for gold. Death strikes him down and the World deceives him by giving his treasure to a stranger, but he dies calling on God for mercy. The Soul prays God to help as the Bad Angel carries him to hell. Mercy and Peace plead for him in heaven against stern Righteousness and Truth, till God the Father orders Mankind saved from the fiend to sit at his right hand.
>
> (*Macro*, pp. xxiv–xxv.)

We shall observe at once that the unknown author (indubitably a cleric) has achieved a skilful fusion of familiar motifs. We may find it harder to answer the question 'What is it all about?', although the title supplied by modern editors, *The Castle of Perseverance*, lays suitable emphasis on the play's unifying theme, the need to persist in virtue till death.

One motif is clearly the Life of Man, conceived as a journey. The journey is bounded by birth and death, and involves Mankind's experience of a series of Ages. In the *Castle*, these comprise a brief innocent childhood; a worldly youth, marked by a first change of costume from 'nakedness' to the 'rich array' of a gallant; penitence in middle age, during which he retires to the sober security of the castle and no doubt puts on appropriately penitential garments; and an old age of reversion to greed and avarice in pursuit of 'more and more'.

A second motif, which supplies much of the central action, is the *psychomachia*, the battle of the soul, derived ultimately from the poem of that name by Prudentius by way of many intervening replays in Latin, French and English. This comprises the Sins' attack on the castle and, by implication, the earlier sinning and repentance which pave the way to it. The Castle itself is an allegorical image of some antiquity and very wide currency, especially during the age of castles (the twelfth to the fifteenth centuries). As readers of Spenser and Bunyan well know, castles in allegory are of many kinds and functions. They may be the dwellings (or embodiments) of the devil, – or of the Virgin Mary, – or, like Spenser's House of Alma, of the human body. The Castle of Perseverance, as the seat of defensive and restorative virtues, carries suggestions of the second and third types. For pilgrims, castles may be destinations: in warfare, they can resist the siege of enemies. Again it is the second class which is most clearly relevant, though – unlike many – this is a castle whose fortifications are not detailed (unless one of the lost leaves contained a passage of description of it). In face of assault, its defences are in any case not military. The weapons of the virtues are red roses, symbolizing the redemptive blood of Christ. The dialogue does suggest one physical line of defence, a moat. This is a feature of several allegorical castles, among them this one described by John Mirk (c. 1415):

> Our lady was as strong as a castle, and resisted the assault of the fiend's machinations. . . . just as a castle has a deep ditch to strengthen it, so has our lady a ditch of meekness so deep down into the earth of her heart, that no man can go over it. . . . If the ditch be full of water, it adds even more strength to the castle; this water is compassion that a man has for his own guilt or for any other man's diseases. This water had our lady, when she wept for her son's passion and for his death so much, that when she had wept all the water that was in her eyes, she wept blood over this ditch, like a drawbridge that shall be drawn up against enemies, and let down to friends that will keep this castle. By this bridge ye shall understand discreet obedience.[2]

Though not a direct source of the *Castle*, *Le Chateau d'Amour*, by Robert Grosseteste (c. 1230), in any of several later English renderings, shows points of similarity. The Castle of Love is a Castle of the Virgin Mary: it has seven barbicans, which are the seven Moral Virtues, and is moated. Man comes to it, in flight from his enemies – the devil, the world, his flesh – and their assistants, and seeks refuge in it. In Passus V of *Piers Plowman*, Truth's dwelling-place is similarly guarded by seven virtues and is reached by crossing the brook 'be-seemly-of-speech' at the ford 'your fathers honoureth':

> Wadeþ in þat water · and wascheth ȝow wel þere
> And ȝe shul lepe the liȝtloker · al youre lyftyme.   *more nimbly*
> (Piers Plowman, V. 577–8)

Crossing the moat can evidently carry the symbolic sense of cleansing, purification or baptism, so that entry into one of the Castles of Virtue can mean 'a transformation of the soul'.

A third motif in the *Castle*, indeed its main theme, more subtly attuned to the play's whole structure, and reflected in the title which modern scholars have given it, is announced in the middle of the play. The 'mother' virtue, Humilitas or Meekness, greets Mankind, on his entry into the Castle, with these words:

> Þis castel is of so qweynt a gynne
> Þat whoso euere holde hym therinne
> He schal neuere fallyn in dedly synne;
>   It is þe Castel of Perseueranse.
> *Qui perseuerauerit usque in finem, hic saluus erit.*
> (1702–6)

'He that shall endure to the end shall be saved' explains the second half of the play's action and accounts for the two points at which the playwright uses the licence of the writer of fiction and takes his audience wholly by surprise. The first of these is the climax of the battle. The Castle resists the blustering military threat of the Devil's sins, Pride, Wrath and Envy, as well as the more insidious tactics of Flesh's team, Lust, Gluttony (with fire) and Sloth (with his spade). These six are pelted with red roses and retire, battered and broken, to endure further blows from their lords. But just as the image of the journey in *Everyman* reverts, with sudden shock, to Everyman's sinking into the grave, so the image of battle in the *Castle* dissolves with moral and psychological conviction into an act of desertion and betrayal from within. The capitulation follows the merely verbal attack of Covetousness, who turns his address away from his natural antagonist, Largitas or Generosity, and appeals directly to his old friend Mankind, who has been out of the action for a long time, though visible behind the defensive line of virtues.

Auaricia How, Mankynde! I am atenyde	*grieved*
For þou art þere so in þat holde.	*fort*
Cum and speke wyth þi best frende,	
Syr Coueytyse, þou knowyst me of olde.	
What deuyl schalt þou þer lenger lende	*remain*
Wyth grete penaunce in þat castel colde?	
(2426–32)	

How, Mankynde! cum speke wyth me,	
Cum ley þi loue here in my les.	*leash (control)*
Coueytyse is a frend ryth fre,	
Þi sorwe, man, to slake and ses.	*end*
Coueytyse hathe many a gyfte.	
Mankynde, þyne hande hedyr þou reche.	
Coueytyse schal be þi leche.	*doctor*
Þe ryth wey I schal þe teche	*right*
To thedom and to þryfte.	*prosperity*
(2470–8)	

ȝa, up and doun þou take þe wey	
Þorwe þis werld to walkyn and wende	
And þou schalt fynde, soth to sey,	
Þi purs schal be þi best frende.	
Þou þou syt al-day and prey,	*though*
No man schal com to þe nor sende,	
But if þou haue a peny to pey,	
Men schal to þe þanne lystyn and lende	
And kelyn al þi care.	*assuage*
Þerfore to me þou hange and helde	*hold (obey)*
And be coueytous whylys þou may þe welde.	*as long as you can manage yourself*
If þou be pore and nedy in elde	
Þou schalt oftyn euyl fare.	*live poorly*
(2518–34)	

98

The other moment of shock comes when the Bad Angel, having won a dispute with the Good Angel (much of it, unfortunately, on the second lost leaf), drives Mankind's soul to Hell. It was thus characterized by a reviewer of one recent production of the play:

> what took me completely by surprise was the pathos of the soul. . . . It is obvious in its intention to move and even to frighten, and it uses obvious methods. This production made use too of the obvious (though appropriate) device of having the soul played by a child, and undoubtedly much of the effectiveness of this part depended upon our basic reaction to smallness, apparent innocence, purity and helplessness. It was all obvious, but now I know that it works. And it made emotional sense of the last section of the play: Mankind was both tainted flesh and innocent soul, and whether or not the soul was to suffer had become a matter of paramount importance.[3]

The shock will be compounded for audiences unaware of what is to come. For them, the death of Mankind may carry a sense of finality, though its circumstances should alert them to an unanswered question. Is he damned or saved? He has died in sin, having left the Castle, but he has died with the magic death-bed formula on his lips:

I deye certeynly.	
Now my lyfe I haue lore.	*lost*
Myn hert brekyth, I syhe sore.	
A word may I speke no more.	
I putte me in Goddys mercy.	
(3003–7)	

The Bad Angel has no doubts and is emphatic:

We shull to hell, bothe to,	*two*
And bey *in inferno.*	*in hell*
Nulla est redempcio	*there is no redemption*
For no kynnys þynge.	
(3095–8)	

However, the Soul's cry for mercy is not unheard. It provides the cue for the playwright's introduction of his fourth main motif, the Debate of the Four Daughters of God. This very widespread allegory is expanded from a brief biblical text, Psalms lxxxv.10: '*Misericordia et Veritas obuiauerunt sibi, Justicia et Pax osculate sunt*' (3521). The verse is quoted, in the Latin of the Vulgate, at the end of the play, in the longest speech in it, the plea of Peace for the forgiveness of Mankind by God the Father and for the reconciliation of the conflicting claims of Truth and Mercy, Justice and Peace. In the English of the Authorized Version, it was to become: 'Mercy and truth are met together; righteousness and peace have kissed each other'. As in the *Cas:le*, '*justicia*' is rendered as 'righteousness'. The debate of the four daughters of God, four allegorized attributes of the deity, concerns the need to reconcile the incompatible and absolute demands of Truth and Justice with the loving-kindness and generosity of Mercy and

Peace. It originated in the eleventh century, in Jewish commentary on the Aramaic scriptures, where its occasion was the question whether or not God should create Man. In the Christian tradition, which adopted it later in the eleventh century, the focal question soon changed to become that of fallen Man's redemption. The seminal handling is in the *Meditationes Vitae Christi* (1274), attributed to Bonaventura. The debate entered England about 1200 and it crops up in a variety of forms throughout the medieval period – and indeed much later.[4] As late as 1640–2 John Milton, well embarked on his journey towards *Paradise Lost*, sketched out four drafts of his theme of the Fall of Man in dramatic form. In the third, a prologue by Moses was to be followed by 'Justice, Mercie, Wisdome – debating what should become of man if he fall': in the fourth, Justice and Mercy were to play major roles as, respectively, accuser and comforter of the fallen Adam.[5] More familiar, though no longer overtly allegorical, are the oppositions between justice and mercy in the persons of Shylock and Portia or Angelo and Isabella in Shakespeare's *Merchant of Venice* and *Measure for Measure*.

The only other English medieval treatment of the debate of the daughters of God which is fully and formally dramatic, though lacking the power of Langland's version in Passus XVIII of *Piers Plowman*, is in the *Ludus Coventriae* or N-Town mystery plays. In play 11 the debate of the daughters precedes the Annunciation: the motion for debate is 'Whether or not fallen man should be redeemed – and if so, how?'. This debate leads into a 'Parliament in Heaven', a self-communing of the Trinity:

> *Filius*   A counsel of þe trinite must be had
>   Whiche of vs xal man restore.   *shall*
> *Pater*   In ʒour wysdam son · man was mad thore   *made there*
>   And in wysdam was his temptacion
>   Þerfor sone sapyens ʒe must ordeyn here-fore
>   and se how man may be salvacion.
> *Filius*   Ffadyr he þat xal do þis must be both god and man
>   lete me se how I may were þat wede
>   And syth in my wysdam he be-gan
>   I am redy to do þis dede.
> *Spiritus Sanctus*   I the holy gost · of ʒow tweyn do procede
>   this charge I wole take on me
>   I love to ʒour lover xal ʒou lede
>   þis is þe Assent of oure vnyte.
>   ('N-Town', p. 103, lines 171–84)

The relation of the debate of the daughters of God to the divine decision to redeem man is familiar in pictures as well as in writings of the later middle ages. I stress it merely to highlight the originality of the *Castle* in reassigning it to the question of the salvation of a single soul – although of course the Anima of Humanum Genus both is and is not a 'single soul'.

The play ends with the debate of the four daughters before God the Father *'sedens in trono'*, as umpire, and with his decision to save the soul:

To make my blysse perfyth	*perfect*	
I menge wyth my most myth	*mix*	*might*
Alle pes, sum treuthe, and sum ryth,		
And most of my mercy.		

(3570–3)

As a sparke of fyre in þe se
My mercy is synne-quenchand.
(3602–3)

Equally the play begins with the entries of World, Belial and Flesh, who, between them, outline the situation on earth and state their joint intention to destroy Mankind. The final scene, which may seem, at first, an undramatic excrescence, thus completes a pattern of action as well as concluding the play's argument.

Pattern indeed is a term much needed in discussion of the *Castle of Perseverance*. Its cast of 33 characters comprises Mankind, his Soul and Death, plus two opposing groups, Evil and Good, each made up of fifteen characters. Within these groups are the symmetrical sevens of the Deadly Sins and the Moral Virtues. Actions too are patterned: Mankind twice sinks into sin and twice repents – and each penitence is induced by the stroke of a spear, first that of Penitencia, then that of Death. Mankind perseveres in virtue *in* the castle, and in covetousness *beneath* it. Even the speeches are highly-patterned, not only in their metrical structure and significant use of alliteration, but in their sequence – hardly ever is a stanza divided between two speakers. Thus Mankind exchanges one-stanza speeches with six of the Sins on their first meeting, except that Pride is given two stanzas as first Sin and also as expressing his nature. Similarly, in the battle the odds in favour of virtue are reflected in the imbalance of stanzas – one each for Sins, two for Virtues. Speeches of more than two stanzas are used with great economy: Mankind alone has more than one such speech, and his two are the first and last speeches of his role. Other characters with one long speech apiece are World, Flesh and Belial; Covetousness; Backbiter (the World's messenger); and Confession. All these are in the first half of the play, and all but the last are forces of Evil (though the first missing leaf most likely contained a long speech to introduce the mother Virtue, Humility). In the second half, all but two of the long speeches go, with tidy symmetry, to forces of Good, those for their opponents being limited to Death and to the Bad Angel in his moment of victory, as he drives the Soul to hell. Only the Good Angel lacks a long speech, though once more it could well have come on the second missing leaf, on which he must have made his final plea to save the Soul from hell.

Reading the *Castle* is difficult. The play is long and its style may seem verbose and lacking in variety. But despite the prevalence of 9- and 13-line stanzas, which does encourage repetitiveness, and the reliance – perhaps excessive – on rhyming tags and formulae, the characters are all equipped with styles of speech which, if hardly Shakespearian in their sharpness of individuation, are at least apt to their quality and flexible enough for straight-forward exposition or exhortation as well as for the powerful expression of feeling. The range of contrast available may be best illustrated by comparing the Good and Bad Angels, for instance in their differing reactions to Mankind's initial descent into sin.

Bonus Angelus Alas, Mankynde	
Is bobbyd and blent as þe blynde.	*mocked* *blinded*
In feyth, I fynde,	
To Crist he can nowt be kynde.	
Alas, Mankynne	
Is soylyd and saggyd in synne.	*sunk*
He wyl not blynne	*cease*
Tyl body and sowle parte atwynne.	
Alas, he is blendyd,	*blinded*
Amys mans lyf is ispendyd,	
Wyth fendys fendyd.	*hedged about*
Mercy, God, þat man were amendyd!	
(1286–97)	

Malus Angelus ꝫa, whanne þe fox prechyth, kepe wel ꝫore gees!	
He spekyth as it were a holy pope.	
Goo, felaw, and pyke of þo lys	*pick* *lice*
Þat crepe þer upon þi cope!	
Þi part is pleyed al at þe dys	*dice*
Þat þou schalt haue here, as I hope.	
Tyl Mankynde fallyth to podys prys,	*the worth of a toad*
Coueytyse schal hym grype and grope	
Tyl sum schame hym schende.	*disgrace*
Tyl man be dyth in dethys dow	*put in the grave*
He seyth neuere he hath inow.	
Þerfore, goode boy, cum blow	
At my neþer ende!	
(803–14)	

Physical coarseness is a usual attribute of medieval devils: not surprisingly, the roles of Mankind's three chief misleaders, the Bad Angel, World and Covetousness, invite more informal and animated playing than do their opposite numbers. Mankind too, though never slow to make the audience aware of the significance of his every action, is allowed a relaxed humanity in the sins of his youth – 'We haue etyn garlek euerychone' (1369) – and an answering conviction in his aged devotion to the proverbial wisdom of the wealthy – 'Penyman best may spede' (2671).

The length of the speeches may be adapted to outdoor performance for a large audience – to allow actors to spread their speeches around – but the better one gets to know the text the less likely this explanation becomes. Besides, four hours for a performance timed to start at midday is hardly an excessive playing time, and all the lines are meaningful. On the other hand, syntactic units rarely exceed four to five lines, so that 'scattered' delivery is practically feasible.

The whole setting is an image of the World (= Universe). But verbal detail is also morally significant: explicit disguise of vices as virtues, such as is found in *Wisdom* and in many sixteenth-century moral interludes, is unnecessary when deeper unease can be felt about the ties of loyalty implied when World accepts Mankind as his servant or Covetousness hails him as his oldest friend. The Castle of Perseverance stands in strong implied contrast to Mankind's insatiable desire for 'castel wallys, . . . Wyth hey holtys and hey hallys' (2748–50). These in turn are reduced to the sadly portable 'copboard' which represents his wealth in old age.

There remains the question of staging. Though a diagram which is obviously concerned with the matter is present in the manuscript, we do not certainly know that the play was ever performed in the fifteenth century. The presence of the 'banns' which precede the text would clearly suggest that performance was at least intended, although their relation to the text raises some questions and they may be of substantially later date than its composition. They are designed to advertise the play one week before a performance.

> Grace if God wyl graunte us of hys mykyl myth,   *might*
> Þese parcellys in propyrtes we purpose us to playe   *parts in fit manner**
> Þis day seuenenyt before ȝou in syth   *sight*
>   At . . . on þe grene in ryal aray.
> Ȝe haste ȝou þanne þedyrward, syrys, hendly in hyth,
>   All goode neyborys ful specyaly we ȝou pray,
> And loke that ȝe be there betyme, luffely and lyth,   *light*
>   For we shul be onward be vnderne of þe day,   *afternoon*
>   Dere frendys.
>
>   (131–9)

The first surprise is that so vast a play should be intended for touring: the blank space in line 134 is evidently intended to accommodate the name of any proposed place of performance. Even with doubling, the minimum cast required is twenty-seven, and the costumes, properties and necessary elements of the staging add up to a very substantial load of luggage (as the visits of the 1978 London production of the play to churches outside London, which required the services of a large truck and a team of stage hands to transport the Castle and scaffolds, amply demonstrated). Clearly

---

* The technical sense of properties may also be present.

103

any tour of the *Castle* needs money behind it. In the days before councils and trusts, this money can hardly be imagined as coming from any source but the Church. We must hope that more may one day be learned of the play's auspices, perhaps from the records of a major East Anglian religious foundation (although nothing has yet come to light despite thorough searching of the surviving documents of Lincolnshire and Norfolk, the likeliest counties of origin for the play).

The diagram itself is very well known. Reproductions of it are to be found in all histories of early English drama. Within a ring formed by two concentric circles is a stylized representation of a castle. The top shows courses of stonework surmounted by battlements. It appears to be supported on heavy legs, leaving a clear space beneath it in which is portrayed a bed. Within the ring are four blocks of words. Above the castle they read:

> þis is þe castel of perseueraunse þat stondyth In þe myddys of þe place, but lete no men sytte þer, for lettynge of syt, for þer schal be þe best of all.

below it:

> Mankyndeis bed schal be vndyr the castel and þer schal þe sowle lye vndyr þe bed tyl he schal ryse and pleye.

while on either side of the bed, awkwardly divided, are the cryptic lines,

> Coveytyse copbord   schal be at þe ende
> be þe beddys feet   of þe castel.
> (*Macro*, p. 1).

Thus the location of the three large properties, or components of the set, is exactly prescribed. The site of Mankind's death lies beneath the refuge of his penitent years: the portable 'copbord' which an unknown heir will wrest from him on his deathbed stands in immediate contrast to the size and strength of the castle which represents the play's spiritual values as well as the image of Mankind's worldly ambitions.

Outside the ring, five brief notes give the orientation of five scaffolds: south is at the top. They read, clockwise: '*Sowth Caro skafold*', '*West mundus skaffold*', '*Northe Belyal skaffold*', '*Northe est Coveytyse skaffold*', and '*Est deus skaffold*'. The placing of God in the east and the Devil in the north is traditional, leaving south and west for the devil's two fellow Evils, the Flesh and the World. That Avarice should have his own scaffold not only underlines the key role played by this sin in the action but provides a location for the convivial meeting of Mankind with the rest of the deadly sins. God's scaffold remains unused until the final scene, by which time, in any open air afternoon performance, the sun will have moved far enough to the west to allow for the possibility of strong lighting of God.

Between the two circles of the enclosing ring is written:

þis is þe watyr abowte þe place, if any dyche may be mad þer it schal be pleyed, or ellys þat it be strongly barryd al abowt, and lete nowth ouyrmany stytelers be wythinne þe plase.

What the ring represents remains a chief point of controversy. In his brilliant reconstruction of the staging of the play,[6] Richard Southern took it to be the outer boundary of the area which contained both playing place and audience. More recent investigators tend to see it rather as representing the moat of the castle and also serving as a barrier to separate the castle and the space immediately beneath it from the rest of the action as well as from the incursions of spectators.[7] Both hypotheses have their difficulties. Southern's ditch, with the mound of earth inside it supporting scaffolds and audience alike, seems impossibly costly in terms of hire of labour and expense of time: conversely, the ditch could only complicate the action by rendering the space described as 'the best of all' difficult of access, which it only needs to be in the central scene of the siege of the castle by the sins.

The remaining words are below the diagram:

and he þat schal pleye belyal loke þat he haue gunnepowdyr brennynge In pypys in hys handys and in hys erys and in hys ars whanne he gothe to batayl.

þe iiij dowterys schul be clad in mentelys, Mercy in wyth, rythwysnesse in red altogedyr, Trewthe in sad grene, and Pes al in blake, and þei schul pleye in þe place altogedyr tyl þey brynge up þe sowle.

These two sentences add a final touch of detail about costume and business which helps to sharpen our sense of contrast between the heavenly and hellish contingents. Red for Righteousness (Justice) is conventional, as is the use of fireworks for stage devils.

Richard Southern stated his claim that this diagram represents a 'medieval theatre in the round' in the very title of his book. The question remains, however, whether the diagram itself is more properly to be seen as representing a theatre or the set for a particular play. That staging in the round was one of the familiar techniques of medieval drama is amply attested by the evidence of other plays, notably the Cornish *Ordinalia* and *Meriasek*, which likewise contain schematic diagrams of a less pictorial kind indicating the orientation of scaffolds or mansions for some principal characters or locations. In Cornwall, traces still exist of circular arenas, of which at least two are substantially complete and may be correctly associated with documentary evidence of playing in the round in the later middle ages, and even as late as the early seventeenth century. The so-called *Ludus Coventriae* or N-Town mystery plays have stage directions which imply circular staging for the sequence of plays that covers the events of Holy Week.

But among the various kinds of evidence adduced for playing 'in the round' in medieval England, the *Castle of Perseverance* diagram has one unique interest: it describes a setting which, whatever interpretation of its details may be offered, is clearly intended as an intrinsic part of the allegory of the play. The point was sharply made by Peter Meredith, in his review of the 1978 production in the Church of St. Bartholomew the Great in London – a setting which could not reproduce the spacial relations demanded by the diagram, and which consequently lost some of the play's sense of ironic juxtaposition of actions. He wrote that in *The Castle of Perseverance*, ' "theatre" and play are one. The circle of evil with only one route for escape; the central point of refuge, by which Mankind starts, to which he comes, from which he is drawn away, and by which he dies; the probably closed and certainly silent heaven which no one can know till after death; all these symbolic meanings are physically present in the setting'.[8]

Revivals of *The Castle of Perseverance* face one major decision, on which some part of the meaning that will emerge from the play must depend: whether or not to attempt a physical approximation to the circular setting (and by implication auditorium) of the diagram. Recent productions which made the attempt include two by Philip Cook, one in the cloisters of Abingdon Priory in 1974, the other indoors at the drama department of the University of Manchester in 1981; and an open-air production by David Parry on the green in front of University College, Toronto, in 1979. The two out-of-doors productions exploited the lighting effects of different times of day, Cook's starting in the early summer evening and continuing by artificial light well beyond nightfall and Parry's starting at 2.30 and ending at 7.30. Both these productions constructed a central castle big enough to hold the virtues and Mankind – in Toronto it had two stories and a retractable ladder – and the five scaffolds required on the circumference of the playing space. Their audiences, whether seated (Abingdon) or free either to sit or to move about (Toronto), filled the segments between the scaffolds. The central 'place' remained free for the actors, although their freedom of movement was limited at Toronto by the stylized representation of a ditch surrounding the castle (which was crossed by a bridge and which Sloth, as his lines require, duly breached with his spade during the siege). The ample space around the playing area at Toronto was used for large-scale processional effects such as an initial entry for World on the back of an artificial horse: such effects would help to account for the five-hour playing time.

Productions which adopted other settings included one by students in the gardens of Trinity College, Oxford, in 1957 and another, directed by Howard Davies, in the summer of 1978, which played first in the church of St. Bartholomew the Great in Smithfield and then toured to give single performances in St. Alban's Cathedral, Tewkesbury Abbey, Romsey Abbey and Southwark Cathedral. My distant memories of the Oxford

Plate 7: *Mankind with the Virtues: aerial view from the production of The Castle of Perseverance by the Poculi Ludique Societas, 1979.*

production (which shared a double bill with the Wakefield Second Shepherds' Play and must therefore have used a severely curtailed text) include strong images of the emblematic costuming of the seven deadly sins and of the final appearance of God on top of a garden wall which had earlier served for the castle. Though impressive in itself, the open-air staging thus removed two crucial phases of the action, the siege and the pardon of the soul, to a place as remote as could be from the seated audience, as well as sacrificing the special effect of anticipation created by the presence of the silent and unused scaffold of God. Covetousness, a lean, black, miserly figure, rose to the opportunity of his big scene, making his seduction of Mankind from the castle into the climactic reversal it should be. The main drawback, namely the relative lack of audience involvement, was highlighted by contrast with a happy moment during the Shepherds' play when the mature midsummer lamb borrowed for the occasion leapt from the cradle and was only cornered after a general hue and cry in which cast and spectators joined with equal enthusiasm.

Circular staging makes graphic, as no other can, the progress of Mankind to each of the play's structures in turn (except Flesh's scaffold) and especially the contrast between the living man's repeated journeys to and from the castle and the single decisive course of the soul to hell and back again to God's scaffold. Something of the sense of mobility was indeed achieved by Davies, who placed his castle (which also served as a stage for the birth and death of Mankind) at the east end of the nave, in the form of a raised platform with seven arches for the seven virtues to defend. The scaffold of Covetousness was on the north side of the nave, about three-quarters of the way from the castle to Hell-mouth (at the west end of the church). The World and the Flesh faced each other across the nave midway between the castle and hell. The audience was seated down the two sides of the nave, between the scaffolds. This arrangement worked well for the play's many journeys and allowed great freedom of movement to such figures as Backbiter, World's messenger, and the Bad Angel. Its disadvantage was that longer passages played on or near a single scaffold, like Mankind's first stay with Covetousness or the siege of the castle, left many spectators feeling remote from the action and having difficulty hearing the lines (a problem eased neither by the resonant acoustic of the larger churches nor by the masks worn by Belial and the Seven Deadly Sins). The pursuit of the soul, played by a small, white-robed boy, down the whole length of the nave by the exultant Bad Angel was a moment well served by the church setting. The director's most radical innovation was to follow, an innovation devised to compensate for the lack of space for a scaffold for God. Mercy, attracted by the soul's cries, came into the nave followed, from different directions, by her sisters. On their decision to take the case up for divine arbitration, they led the whole audience (suitably encouraged by 'sticklers') from their seats to the Lady Chapel (or high altar) where God, in papal triple crown, was awaiting them. After the redemption of the soul, it was the turn of the Bad Angel to flee howling to hell down the whole length of the darkened church.

Another expedient for the staging of the final scene in a confined space was devised for the Manchester production. It was thus described by David Mills in a review of the production: 'as the climactic surprise effect, the upper stage above Hell-mouth opened, to reveal a tableau of God in glory with the Virtues and Good Angel, to which Mankind was appropriately to ascend'.[9]

Commentary on modern revivals of *The Castle* identifies two main areas of difficulty: the achievement of adequate rapport between play and audience, and the striking of an acceptable balance between its antithetical qualities of spectacular impressiveness and subtlety of detail. None of the productions to which I have referred seems to have found consistently satisfying solutions, although circular staging clearly offers the best circumstances for close contact with an audience, especially if that audience is allowed some freedom to move. Nor should the barrier imposed by the play's style, and especially its metre, be underestimated: the task of speaking the lines not only intelligibly but with some immediacy of feeling and personal inflection has understandably proved beyond the capacity of many of the amateur players who have provided most of the modern casts. Yet it has been the experience of many spectators of these and other revivals that the play retains its power to impress. My own most vivid memory of the play in performance is certainly testimony to its power over a mixed and non-specialist audience. At Abingdon (where the performers were professionals working together on the production in their summer holiday) the death of Mankind and the driving of the soul into a luridly lit and densely devilled Hell-mouth took place after dusk. For a moment, the audience was shocked into silence and perceptible confusion: many evidently thought that this was the end of the play and they didn't know how they were expected to respond. The arrival of Mercy brought audible relief, and the debate of the daughters of God was launched with all that urgent particularity which distinguishes dramatic action from philosophical discussion.

Plate 8: *Facsimile of a woodcut from the Basle edition of* The Ship of Fools *(1494).*

> *His points of pride, his eyelet-holes of ire,*
> *His hose of hate, his codpiece of conceit,*
> *His stockings of stern strife, his shirt of shame,*
> *His garters of vain-glory gay and slight,*
> *His pantofles of passion will I frame . . .*
>   Sir John Davies, *A Gulling Sonnet*

'Lusty fresche galaunts'

Tony Davenport

To be young in the medieval drama is to be weak, wayward and wrong, usually in that order. In both mystery and morality plays the emphasis is on man's fallen nature and suspicion and censure are directed towards enjoyment of the pleasures of the body and of the merely temporal. The treatment of human life in the allegorical plays particularly tends towards the generalized and patterned./Youth is seen as a time of mistaken confidence in natural life, or 'the pride of life'.[1] Traditional proverbial wisdom puts it thus:

> Ald man witles
> Yung man recheles   *heedless*
> Wyman s(h)ameless
> Betere ham were lifles.
>   (Robbins, p. 328)

This is a version of a poem surviving in nine or ten manuscripts listing 'Five Evil Things', itself a variation on a familiar moral commonplace of medieval homilists and satirists concerning the 'Twelve Abuses of the Age'. In such lists the heedless folly of young men is the main subject of reproof. The heedlessness is the refusal to accept the wisdom of older generations; the young man is characterized as '*adulescens sine obedientia*' (the disobedient youth, the prodigal son) but this figure is often fused with another of the twelve abuses, '*pauper superbus*' (the penniless and proud, the 'needy nothing trimm'd in jollity', as Shakespeare identifies him), to form a composite of vanity and impiety, the proud gallant.

The imagery of clothing is an important way in which expression is given to the contrary states of the soul in medieval writing and it is especially significant in plays.[2] Innocence and honesty wear long, concealing robes of sober cut. Instances are the 'syde gown' in *Mankind* which in the course of the play New Guise has cut down to a jacket of the new fashion, and the ample clothing in which Lucifer sees Mind, Understanding and Will in *Wisdom*; 'Change þat syde aray', he recommends and the change is into fashionable young man's dress, typical of the exaggeratedly modish

111

costumes which signify worldliness and sin. Man glorifies his flesh by assuming the trumpery finery of the world or of the court, and flaunts his short gown and immodest codpiece, his wide sleeves, his striped hose, his lace trimmings, the elegant, smooth tightness of his hose, his open shirt, his slashed doublet and sleeves 'Disguysed and jagged of sundrie fashion'. With the costume goes an attitude:

> Lo, here is a ladde lyght,
> Al fresch I ʒou plyght,   *assure*
> Galant and joly.
> (*Non-Cycle Plays*, p. 121)

says Delight in a fragment of a play; it is enough to identify the role. The key words 'lyght', 'fresch', 'galant' and 'joly' are as sure a sign of the debauched prodigal as the stage direction in the later interlude *Like Will to Like*: 'Tom Tospot commeth in with a fether in his Hat'. A host of examples presses on us the association between colourful dash in costume and irresponsibility, newfangledness, empty display and foolishly merry behaviour. The return to a state of redemption may be signified by the assumption of a penitential garment: 'a garmente of sorowe' is given by Knowledge to Everyman; 'Hold here a new garment/And hereafter live devoutly', says Contemplation to Free Will in *Hick Scorner*; in *Wisdom* Anima's return to her original garb of 'wyght clothe of golde gysely purfyled wyth menyver' (elegantly trimmed with fur) marks her restoration from the state of corruption signified by an appearance 'in þe most horrybull wyse, fowlere þan a fende'.

Though the word 'galaunt' may signify merely 'a man of fashion', its sense is most frequently pejorative. 'Voyde all dronkelewes, lyers and leechours . . . Gallantes, dise-pleyers and hasardours', says Lydgate in his *Dietary*, and it is in the company of tavern-haunters and scruffy hangers-on aping the manners of the nobility that gallants often appear. Such characters are, of course, familiar, before the word 'gallant' became current, in English satires on 'the way of the world nowadays' from the thirteenth century onwards.[3] 'Satire on the Retinues of the Great' (1307) scathingly identifies the 'gedelynges', 'gromes', 'harlotes', 'hors-knaves', pages and lads who

> . . . boskeþ huem wyþ botouns, ase hit were a brude,   *adorn themselves;*
>   *bride*
> wiþ lowe lacede shon of an hayfre hude . . .   *heifer's*
>   (Robbins, p. 28)

that is, who waste their substance on vanity above their station; spendthrift pride is contrasted with the sordid picture of these horse-holders waking up lice-ridden, scratching their scabs. The technique of 'satirising' by juxtaposing pretentious finery and humiliating physical detail is one that play-wrights imitate.

Later in the fourteenth century such types begin to be called 'gallants'. An early instance is a picture of Richard II's favourite Robert de Vere taking flight, with Michael de la Pole, into a seedy Continental exile in 1388:

> Galauntes, purs penyles
> > *per vicos ecce vagantur;*   *through the city-streets see they wander*
> Yf yt be as I gesse,
> > *male solvunt quod mutuantur.*   *they ill repay what they borrow*
> > (Wright, Vol. I, p. 274)

The poet goes on to envisage the loose life of the social parasite, now here, now there, with 'lytel or noght in her powch' but always 'fresch of the newe towch', with padded shoulders, wide, high collars, long spurs on their heels and the tight-drawn hose which makes it impossible to kneel or bend. The literary ancestry of the figure is betrayed by the poet's mockery of gallants as lovers, burning in ice and toasting their mistresses:

> 'Vive la belle!' thei cry
> > *fragrantia vina bibentes.*   *drinking sweet-scented wines*
> > (p. 277)

There are many echoes of this type of satire on manners and costume in the lyrics of the fifteenth century.

A particularly attractive example is the carol with the refrain:

> Huff! a galawnt! *'Vylabele!'*   *'Vive la belle'*
> Thus syngyth galawntys in here revele.
> > (Robbins, p. 138)

This is an economical expression of all the main ideas which are more lengthily moralized upon elsewhere. A touch of allegory at the start reminds us of the moralizing, satirical tradition that sees the gallant as a sign of the decadence of the times, an instance of the pride of life:

> Galawnt, pride thy father ys dede;
> Thow hast hym robbyd, as y rede,
> And clothyd the in galawntes wede –
> > Huff! a galawnt!

A series of familiar criticisms of costume and vanity follow – the tight-fitting hose splitting at the knee, the showy stomacher at the front and the torn shirt at the back, the long-toed shoes, the shirt cut low to show the chest, the short tunic, the empty purse, the long hair, the mixture of gaudy colours – the whole worthless vagabond. But the jaunty rhythm of the rhyming lines and refrain and the brief taunts and descriptions are lively and light-hearted in effect. The chorus of song 'Vylabele!' is a neat expression of the gay insouciance of the gallant as serenading lover, echoing the 'Vive la belle' of the earlier macaronic lyric. Ironically the refrain of this carol was itself to become an identifying catchphrase. Originally a falconer's cry to flush the prey from cover, *Huff* (or *hof* or *huffa*) passes over from the voice of the falconer-satirist in this poem to the victim and becomes a sign of the gallant's trivial mirth. In *Mary Magdalen* Curiosity enters with:

> Hof, hof, hof! A frysch new galaunt!

Riot in *Youth*, Imagination in *Hick Scorner*, Courtly Abusion in *Magnificence* all similarly enter huffing. Only in *Nature* is the phrase given to a commentator, when Pride devises the transformation of Man. The currency of the phrase and its variations is clearly indicated by the pop-song doggerel appearing as a marginal scribble in the Macro manuscript (in the text of *Wisdom*):

> Wythe hufa
> Wythe huffa w^t huffa w^t huffa onys agen
> A gallant glorius.
>> (*Macro*, p. xxix)

The catchword is still remembered in later plays – *The Four Elements, Three Ladies of London, Histriomastix.*

    Comments on extravagant costume of a much more heavy-handed type than in the Rawlinson quip[4] appear throughout the fifteenth century in works teaching manners and morals, and by mid-century the type-figure of the gallant had become familiar in such writing. The tale of a gallant knight punished for vanity in Peter Idley's *Instructions to his Son* (composed probably 1445–50), and the description of 'ruskyn galaunte' in the later translations of *The Book of Curtesye* show an interest, characteristic of such combinations of religious teaching and etiquette, in spicing advice with illustrative examples.[5] The combination of exhortation and exemplum is a strong connecting thread between instructive manuals and a morality play such as *Mankind*, which was written at about the same time as Idley's work and possibly draws on it as well as on other manuals of sin such as *Jacob's Well*. The 'gallantry' in this play consists of persuasion by the three vices, New Guise, Nowadays and Nought, of Mankind to abandon his long working robe and set off for the tavern; he becomes a figure of fun not because of any flaunting of rich excess but merely for the exchange of a modest, sensible garb for an immodest, foolish one. The relationship between Mankind and Mercy in the play is exactly that of the apprentice and the instructor in manuals such as Idley's; handbook has become drama simply by the invention of dialogue between the two. As with the manual, the imaginative life of the play is in the illustration and exemplification of a course of assaults by evil on virtue, of weakening resolve and of the consequences of sin.

One of the most thorough moralistic treatments is a substantial fifteenth-century poem known as 'A Treatise of a Galaunt' (or 'A Song of Galaunt') which survives in both manuscript and printed editions of varying length.[6] The poet sees 'our Englysshe nacyon' consumed by 'newe dyssymulacyon'; pride disfigures nature, leads men to imitate the French and destroys the chivalry, manhood and profitable trade of England's former glory. In the idea of the gallant is concentrated all sin and the very word becomes a symbol for the decay of the 'world nowadays':

> For in thys name Galaunt ye may se expresse   *explicitly*
> Seuyn lettres for som cause in especiall,
> Aftyr the seuyn dedly synnes full of cursydnesse,   *according to*
> That maketh mankynde vnto the deuyll thrall.
> Was nat pryde cause of Lucyferes fall?
> Pryde ys now in hell, and Galaunt nygheth nere.
> All England shall wayle that eure came he here.
>
> G for glotony that began in paradyse.
> A for Auaryce that regneth the world thorough.
> L for luxury that noryssheth euery vyce.   *lechery*
> A for Accydy that dwelleth in towne and borough.   *accidie (sloth)*
> V for Wrathe that seketh both land and forough.
> N for noying Enuy that dwelleth euery-where.
> T for toylous pryde: these myscheuen oure land here.   *troublesome*
>
> (A, 57–70)

The last two letters give some trouble in the acrostic and the printed editions leave out this stanza and go straight on to a more detailed listing of aspects of sin following the letters of the word. So the 'gay galaunt' can be linked by alliteration not only to the frequently ascribed qualities of guile and 'jettynge' but also 'gabbynge and glosynge'. The arbitrary but ingenious logic of the letter fuses avarice, ambition and arrogance, sees lechery, lust and liking as the cause of loss of love and law, and condemns *accidie* as a force of Antichrist and cause of adversity. The power of the poem is concentrated in these stanzas about sin. Alliteration creates a series of balancing, interlocking patterns; sin may be seen as stemming from and leading to other evil or, on the other hand, as an antithesis to virtue. So if the 'wanton werynge of clothes' is the symptom of 'wastynge and vanyte', 'nycete', 'newe fangles' and 'neclygence' are seen in antithesis to what they have perverted – the 'noble course of nature'. By the interplay of similitudes and contraries the gallants become the centre of a gallery of figures from which the scenes of morality plays could be composed.

> For trygetours and tryflours that tauernes haunt   *tricksters*
> Haue trouth and temperaunce troden vnder foote.
>
> (B, 106–7)

This is not far from a synopsis of the first half of *Hick Scorner*, for instance.

> Pryde goth before and shame cometh behynde
> (B, 200)

the poet sums up – and Barclay was content to echo him in his version of the world as a collection of fools and knaves in *The Ship of Fools*. In the concentration on the gallant in this poem we can see the figure as symbolic of the world and of man in the world as he is displayed in the morality plays. Not only is the gallant an aspect of man, a stage in his youthful folly, but he is an expression of a whole nexus of the social and moral failings of the contemporary world in the suspicious eyes of the moralist looking for the traditional English virtues, for sober modesty, plain simplicity, truth without cleverness, honest permanence.

> All people laboure of this newe dysguysynge
> In forgynge theyr fantasyes to maynteyne pryde.
> He is nowe wysest that can moost of deuysynge;   *knows most about*
> Good makynge of a man is nowe layde on syde.
> (B, 176–9)

By 1500 the gallant is a set character in literary satire. Barclay's version of *The Ship of Fools* includes a powerful chapter 'Of newe fassions and disgised garmentes' in which he invents much to supplement the Latin and French versions that he used as his base. A bold summons sets the satirical tone:

> Draw nere ye Courters and Galants disgised
> Ye counterfayt Caytifs, that ar nat content
> As God hath you made . . .
> Unstable is your mynde: that shewes by your garment.
> A fole is knowen by his toyes and his Cote.
> (Barclay, p. 35)

Economically gathered here are elements that look both back and forward – the falsification of nature, mutability indicated by newfangledness and the association of the gallant and the fool in motley, which is to appear in later Tudor plays. Barclay elaborates these themes in lively pictures of young gentlemen who 'go ful wantonly in dissolute aray'. The end of many such is the French pox or the gallows:

> At Newgate theyr garmentis ar offred to be solde.
> Theyr bodyes to the jebet solemly ascende,
> Wauynge with the wether, whyle theyr necke wyl holde.
> (Barclay, p. 37)

The ideal in sober garments is offered in contrast:

> But ye proude Galaundes that thus yourselfe disgise
> Be ye asshamed. Beholde vnto your Prynce.

Consyder his sadness: His honestye deuyse;   *sobriety*
His clothynge expresseth his inwarde prudence.
(Barclay, p. 39)

The work was printed after the accession of Henry VIII, but this probably refers to Henry VII, though, as Barclay's contemporary Skelton shows, calls to Henry VIII to observe measure could be a useful satirical ploy.

Skelton himself contributed some sharp variations to 'gallant' literature. His opponent Garnesche gets the word as a taunt:

Huf a gallant Garnesche, look on your comely corse!
Lusty Garnesche, like a louse, ye jet full like a jasp;
As witless as a wild goose . . .
('Against Garnesche', II, 16–18)

A more detailed and more vivid account is that of Riot in *The Bowge of Court*:

Wyth that came Ryotte, russhynge all at ones
A rusty gallande, toragged and torente,
And on the borde he whyrled a payre of bones: *a set of dice*
'Quater treye dews' he clatered as he wente.   *i.e. 4, 3, 2*
(344–7)

Skelton's pointed expression makes far more of the material than·do many other of the poets quoted. Riot is a bleary-eyed reveller, the descendant of the 'purs penyles', flaunting the shabby ribaldry of the stews rather than the gaudy fashions of the court. Even so, when, in this semi-dramatic dream-poem, Skelton gives him his own monologue, it is as the reckless spokesman of sensual earthly life:

And, syr, in fayth, why comste not us amonge
To make the mery, as other felowes done?
Thou muste swere and stare, man, aldaye longe,
And wake all nyghte and slepe tyll it be none;
Thou mayste not studye or muse on the mone.
This worlde is nothynge but ete, drynke and slepe,
And thus with us good company to kepe.
(379–85)

Not since Langland's portrait of the recklessness of life has personification so richly and clearly defined attitudes and moral status. In this sort of realization of a character type dream-poems could, in my view, be psychologically more flexible than morality plays, in which the psychological interest is more likely to be in the antithesis between contrasting types or in the composite picture of human nature. The use in the plays of a central mankind figure who represents the whole, where the other allegorical characters are only a part, places a changing figure against pieces of fixed behaviour chosen to illustrate aspects of human morality. In *The Bowge of*

117

Court Skelton's narrator is Drede, in whom we can see an aspect of ourselves. In *Magnificence* his centre is the larger figure of the King of Life, both ruler and human nature; for him the gallant's guise is a more detachable, externally imagined possibility than it appears in the vivid, subtle figure of Riot.

Two things emerge from this brief review of some of the appearances of the gallant in late medieval verse: first, there is a large body of material which establishes the figure as a type, on which playwrights drew; secondly, the figure was variously used and could be handled with originality by individual writers. In the plays too one finds variety in the use of the conventional *topos*, plus, quite often, a double-edged, ironic quality. As a fifteenth-century poet points out, if money 'maketh the galaundes to Iett' (strut), it also creates 'Justynges, plays, dysguysynges' (Robbins, p. 135). The link between the gallant's strutting and plays and disguisings is inescapable. The actor, like the gallant, is a flaunter of self. The ambiguity is exploited in Medwall's *Fulgens and Lucrece* through the two 'by-standers' A and B, supposedly members of the audience, who become minor characters within the play as well as commentators upon it. A mistakes B for an actor:

> For I thought verely by your apparell
> That ye had bene a player . . .
>   (I, 49–50)

The reason for the mistake is that life is imitating art and that there is no difference between the pretences of the stage and those of society:

> There is so myche nyce aray
> Amonges these galandis now aday
> That a man shall not lightly   *easily*
> Know a player from a nother man.
>   (I, 53–6)

The gallant turns up in so many plays partly because he provided the opportunity for rich costume display. The character boasts and draws attention to the fashions he is flaunting; other characters continue to focus attention on the costume by condemning it or imitating it. Display goes with contrast, illustration with confrontation. Again, poetry helps us to identify and place the effects used in the plays. There used to be a chantry chapel in Salisbury Cathedral (the Hungerford Chapel, built in the fifteenth century) on the wall of which was a painting showing the confrontation of two figures, a fashionably-dressed gallant and Death, a skeleton in a shroud.[7] With the painting were two rhyme-royal stanzas; the gallant's began:

> Alasse, Dethe, alasse, a blesful thyng þu were
> Yf thow wolldyst spare us yn our lustynesse.

118

Death's response began:

> Grasles gallante in all thy luste and pride,
> Remember þat thow ones schalte dye.

The symbolic representation of the meeting of life and death is given an ironic twist by one's simultaneous perception of the two aspects of the antithesis: vain hope is confronted by unsparing truth, handsomeness by ugliness. A similar irony is likely once one puts words into the gallant's mouth, as the dramatists obviously did, and as another poet did in 'Ye prowd galonttes hertlesse' (Wright, Vol. II, p. 251) by allowing the gallants to answer the accusation and to tax priests with their furred hoods and pleated gowns. The potential moral confusion of allowing the dandy to draw admiration, sympathy or amusement is best used when the boasting is attributed to the Devil.

In the Demon's Prologue to the N-Town First Passion Play Lucifer's 'new engynes of malycious conspiracy' begin with self-display, tempting the audience to the sins and luxuries of the world. The dramatic monologue includes many references which, in order to be fully understood, require a knowledge of satirical pictures of gallants. The initial boast

> Byholde þe dyvercyte of my dysgysyd varyauns
> ('N-Town', p. 227, line 65)

identifies the key ideas of the instability and deceit indicated by several colours and the covering of true nature by a false façade. Again in the next stanza instances (long-toed shoes, crimson hose) are linked to a laconic statement of the motif of upstart pretension:

> Þus a bey to a jentylman to make comparycion.   *lad*
> (71)

The pattern is repeated in the next stanza as the fine holland shirt and the stomacher of cloth of Rennes are set beside another proverbial tag:

> Þow poverte be chef lete pride þer be present.
> (75)

The 'purse with-outyn money' a few lines later repeats the familiar antithesis of the outward show of prosperity and the inner nothing and harps on the motif of falsity. The devil's boasts are used as a lure to catch the audience in the trammels of pride, contentiousness, envy and hypocrisy. The ironical framework for this temptation is provided by shorthand references to the attitudes of 'gallant' satire.

The use of the gallant as a disguise is elsewhere offered as a model to the on-stage representative of man, rather than directly to the audience. This is the case in *Wisdom*. The corruption of the three powers of the soul, Mind, Understanding and Will (the corruption later symbolized as the disfiguring of Anima), is achieved by Lucifer who disguises his own fiendish nature in gallant's garb. Ironically, the illusion of the character's putting on a costume is achieved by the actor's taking one off, as this text's unusually detailed stage directions explain:

> . . . *entreth Lucyfer in a dewyllys aray wythowt and wythin as a prowde galonte* . . .
>
> (*Macro*, p. 125).

The game of changing appearance is one of the main theatrical devices through which morality plays could be physically flexible, and sometimes more revealing of conduct than the actual dialogue. Lucifer's deceit provides the model for man to display his own instability of nature, and though Lucifer's arguments concentrate on persuasion towards the pleasures of an active, worldly life, what he achieves is a change in the outward appearance of the three powers. Disguise and deceit go hand in hand:

> Thus by colours and false gynne
> Many a soule to hell I wyn.
> (547–8)

Though the 'colours' are the devil's rhetorical arts, they also stand for the gaudy costumes in which Mind, Understanding and Will return, the trappings of the world which mask and contaminate the quality of spirit within.

For Lucifer the gallant's façade is a disguise and advertisement; for the powers of the soul it is the sign of and a stage in man's moral decline. As the three powers merrily preen in their 'new aray', proclaiming themselves 'fresch', 'mery', 'jolye' and 'lyght', their mere folly gradually darkens into the sin to which self-glory leads them, Mind into Pride, Understanding into Covetousness and Will into Lechery.

> | To avaunte thus me semyth no schame, | *boast* |
> |---|---|
> | For galontys now be in most fame. | |
> | Curtely personys men hem proclame. | *courtly* |
> | Moche we be sett bye | *valued* |
> | (597–600) | |

says Mind, and his thought soon extends to the tyrannies of the proud lord, to maintenance and oppression and jealousy of others' position. In this highly patterned play the others develop along symmetrical lines, Understanding towards the profitability and deceits of the law courts, to bribery, perjury and simony, and Will towards the sensual satisfactions of reckless extravagance and the City stews. Thus the implications of 'gallantry' are extended and explored, not here through satirical mockery of particular excesses of dress, for *Wisdom* is little concerned with realism, but towards the moral disorder that results from self-indulgence.

Yet a third layer of meaning is exploited when the state of sin into which Mind, Understanding and Will have fallen is identified symbolically through dance and dumb-show. Mind joins six red-bearded dancers to illustrate the worldly forms taken by Pride, Envy and Wrath; Understanding with six hooded jurors mimes the progeny of Covetousness; and Will is joined by three pairs representing Sloth, Gluttony and Lechery performed by six women, 'thre dysgysde as galontys and thre as matrones'. Here the gallant takes his place as a tableau-figure, conveying moral meaning simply by costume and gesture. When the actor thus becomes a representative picture of moral status one finds the nearest visual equivalent to the device of personification.

In *Wisdom* the gallant is thus an aspect that the devil may assume, that man may go through and that in itself can express a moral state. In later Tudor plays the gallant tends to be used less flexibly in the function of minor accomplice to the Devil or Vice. In *Respublica* (1553), for example, Insolence, Oppression and Adulation are called 'gallants', but this is merely to say that they are subsidiaries of Avarice, 'the vice of the plaie'. Earlier the gallant can appear in such a minor comic character-part, as one can see in *Mary Magdalen*. In a kind of play-within-the-play the corruption of Mary is staged by the Devil and the sins. A suitable setting is provided (a tavern in Jerusalem – with tame taverner on hand) and, on cue, the cardboard debaucher enters:

> *Her xal entyr a galavnt, þus seyyng:*
> Hof, hof, hof! A frysch new galavnt!
> (491)

Two stanzas of boasting display his repertoire of shirt, stomacher, doublet and hose and of quips, smirks and sighs. Young (or young-seeming), elegant and lusty, he claims, like others, to 'do it for no pryde!' His name, Curiosity, indicates elegance and ingenuity, preciousness, sophistry and an idle interest in worldly affairs. The neat little pastiche of a courtly love scene between the dandy and Mary is one of the few places in late medieval drama where 'gallantry' involves courtesy and some flourishes of verbal foppery:

> A, dere dewchesse, my daysyys iee!
> Splendavnt of colour, most of femynyte
> (515–6)

says Curiosity and when Mary protests the answer comes glib and sweet:

> *Mari*   Qwat cavse þat ȝe love me so sodenly?
> *Corioste* O nedys I mvst, myn own lady!
>   Your person, itt is so womanly,
>   I can not refreyn me, swete lelly!   *lily*
> (523–6)

The stereotype of the gallant is part of a wide-ranging (though indiscriminately used) dramatic vocabulary of figures, styles and stage effects in this panoramic medley; a mere instrument of the devils and sins who control the action, he is not made to bear any real moral weight.

The combination of show-off character part and of moral function is more significantly visible in the plays of Skelton and Medwall. In *Magnificence* Skelton's chief gallant is Courtly Abusion, who is identified by the opening tag 'Huffa, huffa' etc., and by some sneering ('where had we this jolly jetter?') from fellow conspirators, Cloaked Collusion and Crafty Conveyance, before he is left alone to flaunt his nature. Courtly Abusion preens with the boasts of Youth and Delight:

> My hair busheth
> So pleasantly,
> My robe rusheth
> So ruttingly;   *dashingly*
> Meseem I fly,
> I am so light;
> To dance delight.
>   (834–40)

Satisfaction in the 'new guise' in wide sleeves, well-drawn hose and wide knee-length boots is as near as Skelton gets to any details of costume, but he suggestively and economically covers many of the satirist's stock motifs in his rapid song-like metre – spendthrift excess, French fashions, social climbing, deceit and crime, Tyburn as the end. This scene is a classic example of the morality play's use of display techniques derived from allegorical vision poetry. True, Skelton has welded it into the dramatic texture by using the character's fellow-vices to convey the satirical tone:

> By God, sir, what need all this waste?
>   (754)

says Cloaked Collusion, and

> By the mass, for the court thou art a meet man:
> Thy slippers they swap it, yet thou foots it like a swan.   *flap about*
>   (764–5)

Nevertheless, the essence of the scene is a stand-up monologue.

In the central scenes Courtly Abusion, in the guise of Lusty Pleasure, is given the function of tempting the King with the prospect of a fair mistress, and with the pleasures of wayward wilfulness:

> *Courtly*
> *Abusion*   . . . do as ye list and take your own way.
>
> *Magnificence*   Thy words and my mind oddly well accord.
>
> *Courtly*   What should ye do else? Are not you a lord?
> *Abusion*   Let your lust and liking stand for a law.
>   (1605–8)

This temptation scene gives more weight than hitherto to the idea of the opportunities for recklessness, vanity and self-indulgence afforded by the court. The gallant is a persuasive embodiment of enervating forces which contribute to the downfall of the great. The contrast between the mirth of Courtly Abusion's earlier monologue and the evil of the temptation scene is recognizable as a version of the recurring antithesis between glossy outer appearance and corrupt inner nature, and as an instance of that ironical balance between tongue-in-cheek admiration and moral condemnation that is to be met elsewhere, but to an unsympathetic eye the contrasting facets might suggest that the element of 'merry interlude' in *Magnificence* is at odds with the tragedy of Fortune to which Skelton was giving contemporary significance.

In *Fulgens and Lucrece* Medwall made the antithesis between appearance and reality the debating-point around which the play is organized. The two suitors of Lucrece stand respectively for the nobility of ancestry, inherited wealth and position (Cornelius) and the nobility of 'longe continued vertu', the sober moral life, devotion to God, charity, study and patriotism (Gaius). The aristocrat offers Lucrece riches, ease and idleness, clothes, hunting, hawking, dancing and minstrelsy in contrast to the life he forecasts for her with Gaius: 'a threde bare lyvynge/ With wrechyd scarcenes'. The dramatist's way of illustrating the quality of the aristocratic life is to depict Cornelius as a 'fresshe galant' and to describe the costume of Cornelius and his retinue as proof of his goods and liberality, through his servant B, who is impressed by the cost and amount of material used.

The gallant's uniform has to stand for the claims of castles and towers, treasure and store, and for the snobbery towards social climbing, of which it is elsewhere so often a sign. The satirist's scorn towards the pattern of behaviour that goes with the gallant dress is also given a fresh twist by being attributed to the rival, Gaius:

> He wenyth that by hys proude contenaunce
> Of worde and dede, with nyse aray . . .
> . . . hys ryotouse disportis and play,
> Hys sloth, his cowardy and other excesse,
> Hys mynde disposed to all unclennesse –
> By these thyngis only he shall have noblenesse.
> (II. 634–41)

Complaint of pride in dress has been adapted to serve the argument, inherited from *The Wife of Bath's Tale* and elsewhere, that a life without its own merit cannot claim nobility from that of others. This theme is echoed in later plays: *Calisto and Melibea* and the Rastell/Heywood *Gentleness and Nobility* (both 1527–30).

In *Fulgens and Lucrece* Medwall draws out from the morality play a debating theme about ways of life and enlivens it with the by-play and games of his commentators. Medwall's other play, *Nature*, combines debate with pattern: Reason versus Sensuality and the phases of man's life in the world. 'Gallantry' is part of the development of man, as in *The Castle of Perseverance*, *Wisdom* and *Mundus et Infans*. It is an aspect of Pride, who is the first of Man's 'servants' to come to his aid when he casts off the Innocence of youth and becomes a man 'of the world'. Pride displays his nature in a long boasting speech, flaunting his scarlet bonnet, his long carefully-curled hair and the usual clichés of doublet and sleeves. There is more point in two passages of dialogue concerning fashion. First Pride criticizes Man's out-of-date costume:

> . . . I lyke not your aray:
> It ys not the fassyon that goth now a day.
>   For now there ys a new guyse!
> It ys now two dayes agon
> Syth that men bygan thys fassyon
> And every knave had yt anon!
>   (I. 1023–8)

The turning of satire into this kind of personal conversation gives a more intimate ring to the social comedy. The practised beau and the young apprentice in court-craft are the kind of 'local' variations on allegorical figures that plays for private patrons are likely to produce. The effect is repeated when Pride devises with Worldly Affection, in Man's absence, a suitable garb for the worldly man.

> Syr our mayster shall have a gown
> That all the galandys in thys town
>   Shall on the fassyon wonder.
>   (I. 1058–60)

– with spaces between the seams, a new style doublet without sleeves, fine white shirt, striped hose colourfully trimmed:

> And whan he is in suche aray,
> 'Ther goth a rutter!' men wyll say.
>   'A rutter? Huf, a galand!'
> Ye shall se these foles on hym gase
> And muse as yt were on a mase
> New brought into the land!
>   (I, 1076–81)

: a cavalry soldier, especially German, hence a gay cavalier, a swaggering bully

As with Skelton's use of vices to satirize other vices, so here Medwall finds an ironic touch in Pride's mocking ingenuity as dress-designer and satirist combined. One needs the irony to convert the set-piece display of gallant as comic object into an image of vice which can be a moral thread in a continuously developing dramatic sequence.

The gallant ought, for obvious reasons, to figure largest in plays about the weaknesses of youth, from which I began, but the two early sixteenth-century morality plays which concentrate on the theme, *Youth* and *Hick Scorner*, are slightly unexpected in this respect. *Youth* shows considerable dependence on the kind of dramatic shorthand which I have suggested playwrights developed from the commonplaces of contemporary satire and moral writing. The moral antithesis of the play is stated at the beginning through Charity, who opens, and the challenger Youth, whose boasts include some of the traditional gallant's vanity as well as Pride of Life's glory in health and strength. His arrogant aggression towards Charity is a vivid embodiment of the 'reckless' quality of the allegorical type; with speedy dash the dramatist adds the flippancy of the cheeky boy and the rioter's cursing, and goes on to illustrate Youth's nature through allegory; the three vice figures, Riot, Pride and Lechery, draw out the facets of Youth's sin, before Charity returns and the antithetical challenge continues. It is striking that little attention is given to detailed embodiment of these vice figures; familiarity is assumed and appearance and a few tags are enough. So Riot begins with a quick snatch of the gallant's repertoire:

> Huffa, huffa! who calleth after me?
> I am Riot, full of jollity,
> My heart is light as the wind.
>
> (210–2)

From the quick placing of identity and ancestry he can go gabbling on with anecdotes of Newgate and Tyburn, empty threats and oaths, with no further detail needed to exploit his 'gallantry'. Similarly Pride, to whom the other aspect of the gallant, pride in clothing, is attributed, is characterized by a quick dash through familiar attitudes and advice to Youth:

> Above all men exalt thy mind.
> Put down the poor and set nought by them   *care nothing for*
> Be in company with gentlemen.
> Jet up and down in the way,   *swagger*
> And your clothes – look they be gay.
> The pretty wenches will say then,
> 'Yonder goeth a gentleman'.
>
> (344–50)

But the signs are clear enough without elaboration. The play's editor has found much contemporary reference in *Youth* and argues that it was written for a particular household in late 1513;[8] if he is right, then the play may be seen as a kind of satirical journalism, working as political cartoons do, in recognizable outlines, in caricatures, catchphrases and allusions. But with or without the specific contemporary details, that quality in *Youth* is apparent from late fifteenth-century satirical traditions. With the example of others behind him, the playwright could sketch outlines within which particular Tudor types and even individuals (Henry VIII in the character of Youth, for instance) may be envisaged.

Hick Scorner (1514) borrows from *Youth* and goes further towards specific satire and comic realism. The framework of the reckless young man's trivial, vain life of self-indulgence, petty crime and cocky vanity becomes a vehicle for contemporary allusion and the flavour of the docks and taverns of East London. As in *Youth*, representation of the allegorical stereotype of the flaunting gallant is sketchy, but the brief hints rest on a solid block of material drawn from the satirical tradition to which the stereotype belongs. In *Hick Scorner* there is a particularly striking example of the 'state of England' complaint. Pity, fettered like Charity in *Youth* by the vicious characters, is given a formal lament with the refrain 'Worse was it never!' (lines 546–601). This is based on the commonplaces of the moralist's condemnation of the times:

> We have plenty of great oaths,
> And cloth enough in our clothes.
> But charity many men loathes.
>   Worse was it never!
>   (554–7)

(The first of Henry VIII's statutes directed against 'greate and costly array' defined the amount of cloth to be used in gowns and coats according to rank; the attack is thus historical as well as literary.) The dialogue among the three vicious characters, Free Will, Imagination and Hick Scorner, and the later confessions of the first two provide a catalogue of acts of petty crime, of lechery, of roguery, chicanery, schemes, plots and lies, so that Pity's censure draws together a mass of literal, anecdotal trivia into a justified indictment:

> Courtiers go gay and take little wages;
> And many with harlots at the tavern haunts –
> They be yeomen of the wreath that be shackled   *i.e. the prisoner's*
>   in gyves;   *neck-collar   fetters*
> On themself they have no pity.
> God punisheth full sore with great sickness,
> As pocks, pestilence, purple and axes.   *Such as syphilis, plague,*
>   (586–91)   *purple pustules, and ague*

Hick Scorner is a literary play, drawing not only on the tradition of complaint and on *Youth* but also on *The Assembly of Gods* for its lists of rogues and the mixture of allegory and representative human types of vice, and *The Ship of Fools* (and its derivative *Cocke Lorell's Bote*) for tales of shipwreck and the image of the boat for the dangerous life of the London rogue. Free Will is given an extended metaphorical passage in which the word 'gallant' is, for once, used with some literary subtlety to refer to Tudor ships (the sense still surviving in 'top-gallant') as well as to the dissolute rakes of the town:

For that rock of Tyburn is so perilous a place
Young gallants dare not venture into Kent.
(831–2)

For Imagination, who is given the gallant's opening tag 'Huff, huff, huff!', being light and jolly consists only of the seedy pleasures of tavern and brothel and has little of the panache that imagination might be expected to find in it. Thus the six characters divide into satirists on the one hand (Pity, Contemplation and Perseverance) and the satirized on the other. Display and antithesis form the pattern throughout. The contemporary social and political allusions and the general atmosphere of London low-life turn the play away from moral allegory, in a sense, and yet the mould is the classic Virtue/Vice confrontation and illustration, with the necessary though perfunctory handing-out of a new coat to the converted at the end. The lack of this defining pattern leaves some later plays devoted to the exploitation of social corruption (e.g. *Like Will to Like*) shapeless and blurred.

The gallant is thus of interest not only as a character stereotype and as a characteristic feature of the satirical treatment of youth shared by late medieval poets and dramatists, but also as an instance of the dramatic adaptability of a type-figure with a strongly marked visual identity. The gallant embodied youth versus age, life versus death, body versus soul, appearance versus reality, excess versus measure by flaunting the decorated self. Based on the idea of an assumed façade, the gallant was very much an actor's image, seen with irony in this period of growing self-consciousness about stage illusion. The ironic link between the performance and the play's theme in the idea of disguise reflects the treatment of behaviour in allegorical drama in terms of phases and arbitrary shifts. The gallant is particularly at home in non-realistic drama because of this and I find its use in *Wisdom* especially interesting. Behaviour here is patterned, dance-like, a sequence of guises and steps which creates the effect of a ritualized circle of action returning to the stage picture from which the play began. Something of the same quality occurs in *Mundus et Infans*, where the central figure is repeatedly renamed, as he goes through the phases of the Ages of Man and glories in appearance as young lover (Love-Lust and Liking), 'fresh as flowers in May . . . proudly apparelled in garments gay', and later as King (Manhood Mighty), 'proudly apparelled in *purpur and bice*' (expensive purple and grey cloth). The behaviour is put on with the name and the garment; the play-pattern is a game of moral guises in which man becomes actor of his own history, schematized and turned into visual emblems. More realistic treatment of conduct tends to turn to the satirical exposure of youth's vanity and excess and it is here that the gallant's name and characteristics occur most often. Youth and education are central themes for late medieval plays and for Tudor interludes; from the function of a phase in the allegorical treatment of the education of youth the gallant can easily become in such plays a non-allegorical figure parallel to the central young man. In later plays (e.g. *The Trial of Treasure*, 1567) the gallant is a minor vice or the contemporary of the central character, one of the alternatives for the 'hero' figure, to be discarded or cynically exploited. As such he is apt to be less interesting (though still capable of being interestingly animated as with Osric in *Hamlet*) than his fifteenth-century and early sixteenth-century manifestations as a devil's disguise, man's velvet-and-satin phase or an image of the pretences of stage and of life.

Divine and Human Justice

Robert Potter

In the corrupted currents of this world
Offence's gilded hand may shove by justice,
And oft 'tis seen the wicked prize itself
Buys out the law. But 'tis not so above:
There is no shuffling, there the action lies
In his true nature, and we ourselves compell'd
Even to the teeth and forehead of our faults
To give in evidence.

(Hamlet III. iii. 57–64)

Shakespeare's King Claudius, owing his prosperity to his own guilty acts, ponders the distinction between divine and human justice – the one distant but terrifyingly perfect, the other close at hand and corruptible. His mind conjures up dramatic images, personifying Offence (that is to say, Guilt) in the figure of a rich man of power, shouldering aside a weakling Justice, bribing a susceptible Law with his tainted wealth. In contrast he imagines a frictionless heavenly reckoning, an 'action' (i.e. a trial) in which we ourselves proclaim our own guilt, accusing and condemning ourselves under the compulsion of our own guilty consciences. In these vivid images we may detect not merely Shakespeare's persistently dramatic habit of mind, but also very probably the memory of actual stage events, the presentations of divine and human justice in late medieval drama, still a living reality in the years of Shakespeare's boyhood.

The great themes of the early drama – such issues as sin, redemption, justice and the relationship between God and humankind – transcend the narrow distinctions of genre as well as boundaries of language and nationality. They are exemplified in mystery, saints and morality plays alike, and in Continental as well as English dramas. The art of late medieval drama is, in one sense, the art of objectifying universal ideas in the particularity of dramatic action. In this chapter I hope to show by way of example with what power and compelling subtlety the question of justice is addressed in some of our extant English playscripts.

The late medieval drama takes a decidedly sceptical, and often satirical view of the processes of justice in this world. Earthly justice is seen, more often than not, as a contradiction in terms or a mockery of its own ideals. Those with the worldly power to administer justice, and their obedient underlings, are tainted by that very power, which tempts them to serve their own advantage rather than God's will. The complaints of the shepherds in the Wakefield Second Shepherds' Play focus on the arrogance, lying and villainy of feudal officials who, dressed in the petty authority of painted sleeves and brooches, afflict the poor with such medieval legal abuses as *purveyance* (commandeering of goods in the name of a lord) and *maintenance* (official support of the corrupt practices of subordinates):

> ffor may he gett a paynt slefe/ or a broche now on dayes,
> wo is hym that hym grefe/ or onys agane says!
> Dar noman hym reprefe/ what mastry he mays,   *whatever force he uses*
> And yit may noman lefe/ oone word that he says,   *believe*
>   No letter.
> he can make purveance,
> with boste and bragance,
> And all is thrugh mantenance
>   Of men that are gretter.
>   (*Towneley*, p. 117, lines 28–36)

The central event of the great Corpus Christi cycles of mystery plays is, of course, the Passion of Christ; at the heart of each cycle is an elaborate Passion sequence which encompasses something like a third of the entire performance. In dramatic terms, the Passion fuses two ironically related and antithetical actions – the sacrifice which Christ makes on behalf of humanity, and the simultaneous act of injustice which humanity perpetrates upon Christ. In the N-Town or *Ludus Coventriae* plays (as Peter Meredith has shown) this sequence is set apart as a two-part Passion play, with particularly detailed stage directions which emphasize the theatricality of this act of injustice, and the conscious attempt which the playwright has made to relate the proceedings to his own audience's experience of earthly justice.

While Jesus blesses the populace of Jerusalem, heals the blind and washes the feet of his disciples, on another part of the stage a conclave of worldly power figures conspires against him. The priests Caiaphas and Annas are dressed in the raiment, and furnished with the retinue, of medieval bishops:

> *Here xal annas shewyn hym-self in his stage be-seyn after*   *dressed like*
> *a busshop of þe hoold lawe in a skarlet gowne · and*
> *ouer þat a blew tabbard furryd with whyte and a mytere*
> *on his hed after þe hoold lawe · ij doctorys stondyng by*
> *hym in furryd hodys and on be-forn hem with his staff of*   *one*

130

> *A-stat and eche of hem on here hedys a furryd cappe*   state
> *with a gret knop in þe crowne . . .*   tassel
> ('N-Town', p.230, l. 40 sd.)

As King Lear suggests,

> Thorough tatter'd clothes small vices do appear;
> Robes and furr'd gowns hide all.
> (*King Lear* IV. vi. 166–167)

To these malevolent prelates, and their attendant Doctors of canon law, the playwright adds two civil judges named Rewfyn and Leon 'in ray ('striped cloth') tabardys furryd, and ray hodys a-bouth here neckys furryd' ('N-Town', p. 233, line 80 sd.). These embodiments of the law perceive Jesus' actions as a direct threat to themselves and the law they represent. They determine immediately on a verdict and a sentence.

> *Leon*   þe cawse þat we been here present
> To fortefye þe lawe and trewth to say   enforce
> Jhesus ful nere oure lawys hath shent   overturned
> þerfore he is worthy for to day.   die
>
> *I^us doctor Annas*   Serys ȝe þat ben rewelerys of þe lawe
> On jhesu ȝe must gyf jugement
> Let hym fyrst ben hangyn and drawe   drawn
> and þanne his body in fyre be brent.
> ('N-Town', p. 236, lines 149–56)

Having determined, Mikado-like, upon an execution, these judicial villains arrange for spies to be sent about the country to collect the evidence for a trial. The N-Town playwright's reference to hanging, drawing and burning is of course anachronistic – a bit of contemporary verisimilitude intruded into the biblical narrative. The 'jugement' is indeed the correct fifteenth century punishment for treason: 'the only capital offense under the common law which did not have solely hanging as its physical penalty'.[1] The old critical assumption that such instances are merely naïve or ignorant has given way to a wiser realization of the artful possibilities of such references in catching the attention of a contemporary audience.

Thus a massive miscarriage of justice – by the audience's standards a trumped-up case of high treason – is enacted step-by-step, continuing with Jesus' arrest, and his first examination under torture at the hands of Annas and Caiaphas.

> *here þei xal bete jhesus A-bout þe hed and þe body and*   shall
> *spyttyn in his face and pullyn hym down and settyn hym*
> *on A stol and castyn A cloth ouyr his face*
> ('N-Town', p. 276, line 160 sd.).

The subsequent examination of Christ before Pilate, while following the biblical narrative, emphasizes legalistic manoeuvrings, as Annas and

Caiaphas urge Pilate to pass sentence, and Pilate seeks to evade juris-
diction in the case. The fifteenth century audience would have found a
particular relevance in these machinations; since medieval churchmen
could not be directly involved in punishments requiring the shedding of
blood, they were consequently compelled to seek the co-operation of the
King's courts in bringing heretics and other offenders against the church to
justice. The process at work in this instance resembles the medieval
procedure of *Significavit*, by which a Bishop could apply to the king's
chancery for a writ ordering a lay official (e.g. a sheriff) to imprison or
punish an offender.[2] Thus the N-Town playwright is depicting not merely
an object lesson in the weakness of human nature and human justice, but
also a deeply corrupt struggle between lay and ecclesiastical power. Pilate's
eventual decision to condemn Jesus is shown as a craven capitulation of
fear of popular upheaval and the threats of Annas and Caiaphas:

> *Annas*   ȝa and þou lete jhesu fro us pace
> þis we welyn up-holdyn Alle
> þou xalt Answere for his trespas
> and tretour to þe emperour we xal þe kalle.   *call*
> ('N-Town', p. 292, lines 614–17)

The N-Town playwright carries the act of injustice through to its cruelly
logical conclusion, showing in horrible detail each stage of the legal murder
of an innocent man and compassionate God. If these acts were done to
Christ in the name of justice, he seems to ask, what justice can any of us
expect in this world?

This theoretical question is posed in even more practical terms in the
morality plays. In these dramas, where the action turns on the fate of the
individual Christian soul rather than on biblical narrative, there is more
opportunity to explore contemporary manifestations of law and justice. A
particularly good example is the fifteenth century play *Wisdom*, which may
have been originally presented in an Inns of Court setting.[3]

Like all moralities, *Wisdom* is an exposition of the human condition,
showing in the first instance that mankind, though well intentioned, is
weak and condemned by nature to fall as Adam did. Lucifer, divulging to
the audience his plan for bringing this fall about, expresses it in legal terms.
Man's soul will be made 'reprouable' (l. 537), and at his death

> I xall apere informable   *ready to accuse*
> Schewynge hym all hys synnys abhomynable,
> Prewynge hys Soule damnable
> (539–541).

When the three human mental attributes, personified as the characters
Mind, Will and Understanding, fall under Lucifer's influence, their state of
sin is expressed in visions of sexual license and legal chicanery. At this
point in the play the dialogue, which has been relatively flat and derivative

from its sources in penitential literature, becomes suddenly specific, lively and evocative of a fifteenth century London underworld, where money talks and justice is anything but divine:

Wndyrstondynge And I vse jorowry,	*bribing of jurors*
Enbrace questys of perjury,	*corrupt juries*
Choppe and chonge wyth symonye,	*bargain and barter,*
	sale of ecclesiastical
	preference
And take large yeftys	*gifts (i.e. bribes)*
Be þe cause neuer so try,	*true*
I preue yt fals, I swere, I lye,	
Wyth a quest of myn affye.	*persuasion*
The redy wey þis now to thryfte ys.	*prosperity*
(637–644)	

So speaks Understanding, now re-christened 'Perjury', emerging as a cynical guide to the many easy ways to bend the law. He joins with Mind (now identifying himself as 'Maintenance') to present a veritable Masque of Injustice. This multi-media event features minstrels piping and trumping, costumed dancers, and a mock jury 'The Quest of Holborn' – six two-faced dissemblers, with tell-tale hats to indicate that they have been bribed.

Wndyrstondynge Now wyll I than begyn my traces.	*dance steps*	
Jorowrs in on hoode beer to facys.	*one hood*	*two faces*
Fayer speche and falsehede in on space ys.		
Is it not ruthe?	*a pity*	
The quest of Holborn cum into þis placys.		
Ageyn þe ryght euer þey rechases.	*call out the hounds*	
Off wom þey holde not, harde hys grace ys.		
Many a tyme haue dammyde truthe.		

Here entre the six jorours in a sute, gownyde, wyth	
hodys abowt her nekys, hattys of meyntenance þervpon,	
vyseryde dyuersly: here mynstrell, a bagpype.	*masked*
(717–724 sd.)	

All of this legal satire may serve to flesh out our vague modern notion of the 'Middle Ages' as the hallowed birthplace of English common law, *Magna Carta*, and the courts of Westminster Hall. The script of *Wisdom*, throwing a rather satirical, Dickensian light on such shibboleths, nevertheless shows us, a flourishing human institution – systematic, if corrupt – dedicated to sifting rights from wrongs.

Wndyrstondynge At Westmyster, wythowt varyance,	
Þe nex terme xall me sore avawnce,	*greatly*
For retornys, for enbraces, for	*For returning of writs, for*
recordaunce.	*bribes, for false testimony*
Lyghtlyer to get goode kan no man on lyue.	*more easily*
(789–792)	

133

It remains an interesting coincidence that the growth and development of English legal institutions in the later Middle Ages is roughly contemporary with the proliferation of popular dramatic traditions such as the mystery and morality plays. Can we draw any coherent parallels between these concurrent developments?

The interconnections of drama and jurisprudence are as ancient as the *Oresteia* and as persistent as the ubiquitous trial scenes of television drama. In part this is because judicial processes are inherently dramatic – re-enacting past events for present purposes; moreover dramas are in some senses implicitly judicial – dedicated to reaching a determination of equity and, typically, to distributing punishments and rewards to their fictional participants. This being the case, it is entirely possible that greater cultural connections than we realize may be discerned between the structures of a given society's legal and theatrical institutions. It is worth remembering, for example, that the Ancient Greeks used their theatres for assemblies and courts of law; their rhetorical tradition of education, directed toward litigating in the public courts, clearly had a shaping hand in determining the form and character of their drama.

In the present instance one particular manifestation of English jurisprudence may be observed – the evolution of the jury system, by which an arbitrary and impartial group of citizens came to be charged with the task of re-hearing and determining the facts of a disputed series of events. By the thirteenth century English juries were confirmed in such responsibilities, and their role as judges of fact, hearers of witnesses, determiners of verdicts, continued to expand in the course of medieval and Tudor times.[4] In theatrical terms, a jury is an audience. That English society developed an open judicial system, with an *ad hoc* audience as part of its basic structure (in contradistinction to the closed Continental inquisitional tradition) doubtless had its effects on the concept of many institutions – not the least of which, we may speculate, was the developing English drama. Whatever the actual connections between theatre and law court, there is certainly no shortage of legal references and judicial concerns in the mystery and morality plays.

In the morality play *Mankind*, the author dramatizes the fallen state of his hero by subjecting him to a mock trial, after the manner of a manorial court, in which he confesses the errors of his formerly virtuous way of life, and begs for forgiveness. The judge is the Vice figure Mischief, and the officers of the court are his tempter-assistants Nought, New Guise and Nowadays:

> *Myscheff* I wyll sett a corte.
>   Nowadays, mak proclamacyon,
>   And do yt *sub forma* jurys, dasarde!   *in legal form*
>   *blockhead*

Nowadays Oyyt! Oyʒyt! Oyet! All manere of men
           and comun women
To þe cort of Myschyff othere cum or sen!   *either come or send*
                                           offical excuse
                    (664–668)

Myscheff Mankynde, cum hethere! God sende yow þe gowte!
   Ʒe xall goo to all þe goode felouse in þe cuntre aboute;
   Onto þe goodewyff when þe goodeman ys owte.
      'I wyll,' sey ʒe.
Mankynde I wyll, ser.

New Gyse There arn but sex dedly synnys, lechery ys non,
   As yt may be verefyede be ws brethellys euerychon.   ᴗ. *us rascals*
   Ʒe xall goo robbe, stell, and kyll, as fast as ye may gon.
      'I wyll,' sey ʒe.
Mankynde I wyll, ser.
                         (702–709)

The fall of a morality hero into sin, which often provides the most lively satirical and comic action of the play, is nevertheless a subordinate prelude to the crux of the drama – the hero's recognition of that sin, his repentence and salvation. In dramatizing these crucial moments, the late medieval playwrights show humanity figuratively, and sometimes literally, on trial.

When the hero of *Mankind* comes to his spiritual senses, at the climax of the play, he is so struck by his own guilt that he refuses to believe he can possibly be forgiven. His self-condemnation seems absolute, but the character Mercy – a priest representing God's forgiveness – explains the difference between man's justice and God's:

Mankend The egall justyse of God wyll not
         permytte sych a synfull wreche
To be rewyvyd and restoryd ageyn; yt
         were impossibyll.

Mercy The justyce of God wyll as I wyll, as
        hymsylfe doth precyse: *state definitely*
Nolo mortem peccatoris, inquit, yff he   *'I do not wish a sinner's*
        wyll be redusyble.   *death', he said;*
             (831–834)   *reclaimable*

Here, then, the familiar optimistic conclusion of a morality play is based on a legal insight – one Shakespeare's Claudius might usefully have heeded. Self-accusation does not lead to eternal damnation; rather, if undertaken sincerely while one is still alive, it leads to a royal pardon. Mankind's dawning realization that such forgiveness is possible creates, at the conclusion of the play, a theatrically powerful moment of reconciliation between humanity and the possibility of divine justice.

In *The Castle of Perseverance*, the most elaborately theatrical of the English moralities, the climactic final event of the play is an actual trial scene, in which man's fate hangs in the balance. Mankind has died in a state of sin and, despite his deathbed pleas for mercy, a devil has taken him off across the wide playing space and into Hell-mouth for eternal punishment. His final cries, however, are heard on high – and they provoke the debate between the four allegorical daughters of God: Mercy, Justice, Truth and Peace. Richard Proudfoot has examined the development of this motif in his chapter on *The Castle of Perseverance* above. As he points out, the N-Town dramatization places this event in its traditional theological position, as a prelude to the Annunciation, but the *Castle* playwright changes the setting to a far more compelling dramatic moment. He also turns a theoretical debate into a trial scene; the four daughters, unable to reconcile their divergent views on whether Mankind deserves to be saved, take their case to the highest judge – God the Father, sitting in a throne of judgement on the Heaven scaffold.

An illustration may help us to visualize some of the theatrical possibilities of such a trial scene. A sixteenth century German woodcut (see plate 9) shows the Parliament in Heaven conceived as a trial somewhat similar to that in the *Castle*. In this case the Holy Trinity serve as a panel of judges, with the devil (a monstrous bird of prey) as prosecutor, bringing the defendants Adam and Eve before the bar of justice. Mercy and Peace appear as witnesses for the defence, and Truth and Justice testify for the prosecution. The crucial evidence is also in view – Adam's fall, for the prosecution, and Christ's passion, for the defence.

In the *Castle*, Truth, for the prosecution, argues that Mankind has in truth lived a sinful life and must pay for the consequences ('Lete hym drynke as he brewyth!', 3274). Mercy, for the defence, vividly recalls the passion of Christ and concludes that Mankind must not be lost to hell, since God came to earth in order to save him. Justice (or Righteousness) takes a more severe view of human nature and reminds God that He must obey His own eternal laws:

> *Justicias Dominus justicia dilexit.*   *The God of justice loves just deeds*
> If þou mans kynde fro peyne aquite,
>   þou dost ageyns þyne owne processe.
> Lete hym in preson to be pyth
>   For hys synne and wyckydnesse
>   (3382–3386).

The rhetorical claims of Mercy and Justice seem equally valid and unreconcilable, but Peace is given the final word, and she suggests a solution of reconciliation:

> þerfore my counseyl is
> Lete vs foure systerys kys
> And restore Man to blys,
>   As was Godys ordenaunce.
>   (3518–3121)

Plate 9: *The Trial in Heaven (Bodleian Library (Douce Collection), 133 (387)).*

The reference is to the Old Testament text on which the legend of the four daughters was founded (see above, page 99) which medieval theologians took to be a prophecy of the coming of Christ, and a new concept of divine justice. In place of the severity of the Old Law, there would come a New Law, leavening truth and justice with mercy and peace. It is this definitive idea of heavenly justice which emerges in the climax of the *Castle* trial scene, as God, who has remained judiciously silent during the foregoing pleas, renders his final verdict:

My jugement I wyl ȝeue ȝou by
Not aftyr deseruynge to do reddere,   *according to desert*
                                        punishment
To dampne Mankynde to turmentry,   *damn   torment*
But brynge hym to my blysse ful clere
In heuene to dwelle endelesly
           (3564–3568).

The four daughters, obeying God's decision, invade Hell-mouth, scattering the devil-jailers, rescuing Mankind and bringing him to the Heaven scaffold to sit at the right hand of God the Father. Here the divinity, previously *Pater sedens in trono* ('Father sitting on the throne') in the manuscript becomes *Pater sedens in judicio* ('Father sitting in judgement', 3598). Welcoming Mankind, he ends the play with a vaunting warning to all the estates of society, of a further judgement to come:

Lityl and mekyl, þe more and þe les,	*Humble and mighty*
All þe statys of þe werld is at myn renoun;	*estates*
To me schal þei ʒeue acompt at my dygne des.	*noble throne*
Whanne Myhel hys horn blowyth at my dred dom	*judgement*
Þe count of here conscience schal putten hem in pres	*jeopardy*
And ʒeld a reknynge	
Of here space whou þey han spent,	*How they have spent their time*
And of here trew talent,	*worth*
At my gret jugement	

(3614–3622)

For the late medieval playwrights the realization of heaven on earth, of divine justice unfolding in an earthly context, is the destination and chief end of human history. They did not shrink from staging such wish-fulfilling events, nor did they overlook the dramatic opportunities implicit in such an overturning of the customary structures of human power and authority. Indeed they looked for hints and prophecies of what it might be like. Among the numerous biblical events of Christ's ministry, generally accorded scant attention in the mystery plays, the authors of three of the four extant English cycles focused on an ironic prefiguration of the final judgement, in the story of the Woman Taken in Adultery.

Of the three dramas, the N-Town version is the most detailed, vivid and attentive to the richness of the story's comic ironies. It begins with a scene of Christ preaching repentance and forgiveness, after the manner of Mercy in the *Castle* or *Mankind*. Simultaneously, in another stage locality, a Scribe, a Pharisee and an 'Accuser' – three representatives of the existing power structure (which in this context is Jewish) denounce the upstart Jesus' preaching and its challenge to the legal and social order:

Alas Alas oure lawe is lorn	*6: lost*
A fals Ypocryte jhesu be name	
þat of a sheppherdis dowtyr was born	
Wyl breke our lawe and make it lame	
('N-Town', p. 201, lines 41–44)	

In order to trap Jesus, they devise 'A Ffals qwarel. . . . A ryght good sporte' (lines 57, 66). They will produce a patently guilty criminal and dare Jesus to pardon the offender on the spot. Lacking a malefactor, they contrive a surprise raid on the house of a young and beautiful adulteress, catching her in the act and chasing off her surprised lover:

hic juuenis quidam extra currit indeploydo calligis non ligatis et braccas in manu tenens (124 sd.)
(Here a young man runs out in his doublet, his boots unlaced and holding up his breeches with his hand).

138

They drag the shamed young woman out into the street, and thrust her in the path of Jesus. The corrupt intentions of these upholders of the law could not be more obvious, and what ensues is a contest between two antithetical notions of justice: the letter and the spirit; vengeance versus forgiveness; the Old Law and the New.

The Scribe produces the Mosaic law that prescribes death by stoning for such offences, and dares Jesus to judge her otherwise. Jesus says nothing, merely traces something on the ground with his finger as the accusations go on. When the three plotters ultimately see what he is doing, their conspiracy breaks visibly apart:

> hic ihesus iterum se inclinans scribet in terra et omnes accusatores quasi confusi
> separatim in tribus locis se disiungent   (232 sd.)
> (Here Jesus, again stooping down, shall write on the ground; and all the
> accusers, as if confused, will move apart from each other to three locations).

What has fragmented the conspirators is the sight of their own individual sins, spelled out in damning detail on the ground, prefiguring a final judgement to come in which power and authority will count for nothing, and divine justice for everything. In shame and fear they skulk away, leaving the repentant adulteress alone – and therefore technically unaccused – before Jesus the forgiving judge.

What looms in the future, in the West window of many a medieval church and in the finale of all four English mystery cycles, is not so much a 'Day of Wrath' as a day of equal justice before the heavenly law – a time at the end of time when earthly privilege will be laid aside and due reward given for actions performed, rather than space occupied in the earthly hierarchy. In York, by a telling irony, production of the Last Judgement play was given to the guild of Mercers (that is, merchants) – who were not merely rich enough to stage the elaborate pageantry of the finale, but also presumably most in need of taking its prophetic message to heart. Thanks to recent discoveries we have a good notion of just how elaborate the pageant wagon staging of this event in the streets of York must have been.[5]

The play begins with a prologue in heaven, in which God calls all humanity to judgement:

> Aungellis! blawes youre bemys belyue,   *trumpets at once*
> Ilke a creatoure for to call,
> Leerid and lewde, both man and wiffe,   *learned and ignorant*
> Ressayue þer dome þis day þei schall.
>   (65–68)

At the behest of the angels, in a locality symbolizing earth, the souls of humanity – good and bad – begin to rise from the ground. The good souls are reverent and thankful; the bad souls anguished and self-accusatory. Just as Claudius suspected, they need no prosecutor to wring a confession from them. They realize that their hidden crimes and private sins are now public knowledge:

Oure wikkid werkis þei will vs wreye,	*betray*
Pat we wende never schuld haue bene weten,	*thought* *known*
Pat we did ofte full pryuely,	
Appertely may we se þem wreten.	*openly*
(129–132)	

With the singing of angels, God descends to earth and takes up his seat of judgement. He relates, as if to establish his own credentials for sitting in judgement over humanity, the painful events of his life on earth, culminating in the crucifixion and the passion, and ending with a terrible question:

All þis I suffered for þi sake –
Say, man, what suffered þou for me?
(275–276)

The difference between good and evil, as it emerges in the York *Last Judgement*, is not a question of fine points of doctrine or philosophy, but human compassion; not words – however well-intentioned – but actions. Simply put, the good souls have cared for the unfortunate

Whenne I was hungery ȝe me fedde,	
To slake my thirste youre harte was free;	
Whanne I was clothles ȝe me cledde . . .	*naked*
(285–287)	

while the bad souls have pitilessly abused their power

Whanne I had mistir of mete and drynke,	*need*
Caytiffis, ȝe cacched me fro youre ȝate.	*drove* *gate*
Whanne ȝe wer sette as sirs on benke,	*lords on the bench*
I stode þeroute, weirie and wette;	
(325–328).	

The surprise, for both good and bad souls, is that actions which they performed in a purely human context, and to 'poor naked wretches', as King Lear calls them, turn out to be the ultimate evidence, the final grounds for divine justice. It is a question, in the final analysis, of the identity of God and man:

To leste or moste whan ȝe it did,
To me ȝe did þe selve and þe same.
(363–364)

The late medieval stage astonishes us with its manifested certainties; where we might temporize or equivocate, it states and demonstrates with a pragmatic and optimistic assurance its clear view of what life and death are about. The concluding vision of Heaven on earth, in the mystery and morality plays, is an act of faith in the transcendence of justice in the affairs of men; promising punishment for the heartless cruelty of which humankind was (and is) eminently capable, endlessly vindicating the path of mercy and forgiveness.

NOTES

'Alle hefne makyth melody'
Richard Rastall

1. John Stevens, 'Music in Mediaeval Drama', *Proceedings of the Royal Musical Association*, LXXXIV (1958), pp. 81–95, especially pp. 82–5.
2. JoAnna Dutka, *Music in the English Mystery Plays* (Kalamazoo, Michigan, 1980), pp. 7 f; Richard Rastall, 'Music in the Cycle', in R. M. Lumiansky and David Mills, *The Chester Mystery Cycle: Essays and Documents* (Chapel Hill, North Carolina, 1983), pp. 111–64, especially pp. 120–23.
3. Carolyn Wall, 'The Apocryphal and Historical Backgrounds of "The Appearance of Our Lady to Thomas" (Play XLVI of the York Cycle)', *Mediaeval Studies*, XXXII (1970), pp. 172–92, especially pp. 172 ff. (The play discussed is that of the Assumption, no. XLV in Beadle's edition.)
4. See Rastall, op. cit., p. 135.
5. *REED Chester*, p. 78; *REED Coventry*, passim, especially pp. 208, 216 and 256. A regals was a small reed organ.
6. This was no longer true after about 1530, when the old-style minstrel began to be superseded by musically-literate instrumentalists (such as the Coventry wait James Hewet).
7. I assume *angelic* singing here because of the dramatic context. *Organum* means 'an instrument': hence the plural can mean either 'musical instruments' or a collection of pipes played by a single musician at a keyboard. The verb *cantare*, 'to sing', is used elsewhere in the N-Town plays both for *organa* and for the crowing of a cock ('N-Town', pp. 365 and 277). It is a normal verb for musical instruments: see H. H. Carter, *A Dictionary of Middle English Musical Terms* (Bloomington, Indiana, 1961: Repr. Millwood, New York, 1980).
8. 'Veni electa mea' is the fourth responsory at Mattins on the feast of the Assumption: see S. W. Lawley, ed., *Breviarium ad Usum Insignis Ecclesie Eboracensis* (Surtees Society 71 and 75, 1879 and 1883), II, col. 481.
9. Ruth H. Blackburn, *Biblical Drama under the Tudors* (The Hague, 1971), pp. 50 ff.

Scribes, Texts and Performance
Peter Meredith

1. W. W. Greg, 'Bibliographical and Textual Problems of the English Miracle Cycles', reprinted from *The Library*, 3rd series, V (London, 1914).
2. So far four of the major mystery play manuscripts have been reproduced in the Leeds Texts and Monographs Medieval Drama facsimiles series: two Chester

ones (Bodley 175 and Huntington HM 2), the Towneley manuscript and N-Town. (See Abbreviations.) The York manuscript will be published in 1983, and the third Chester manuscript, Harley 2124, soon afterwards. All folio references in this chapter to the York Register use the new foliation contained in the forthcoming facsimile.

3   *REED* has so far published the records of York, Chester and Coventry. Newcastle-upon-Tyne is due in 1982, and the first part of Norwich in 1983. The Malone Society has published the records of Kent, Lincolnshire and Norfolk and Suffolk. (See Abbreviations.)

4   An edition and full discussion of the manuscript is contained in A. C. Cawley, 'The Sykes Manuscript of the York Scriveners' Play', *Leeds Studies in English*, VII and VIII (1952), pp. 45–80.

5   The antiquarian activity in Chester is briefly described in *REED Chester* pp. xxiii-xxvii.

6   For a discussion of the manuscript see Stephen Spector, 'The Composition and Development˙ of an Eclectic Manuscript: Cotton Vespasian D VIII', *Leeds Studies in English*, NS IX (1977), pp. 62–83.

7   See Peter Meredith, 'A Reconsideration of Some Textual Problems in the N-Town Manuscript (BL MS Cotton Vespasian D VIII)', *Leeds Studies in English*, NS IX (1977), pp. 35–50.

8   For further information about John Clerke and his annotations in the York Register see Peter Meredith, 'John Clerke's Hand in the York Register', *Leeds Studies in English*, NS XII (1981), pp. 245–71.

9   The reference to Isaac is discussed in Meredith, 'John Clerke's Hand', p. 269.

10   For further discussion of the stage directions in the Chester manuscripts see David Mills, 'The Stage Directions in the Manuscripts of the Chester Mystery Cycle', *METh* 3:1 (1981), pp. 45–51.

11   I have here used the forms of the directions from BL MS Additional 10305.

'Apparell comlye'

Meg Twycross

All references to records from Chester, Coventry and York are to the *REED* volumes: since these are arranged chronologically, it has not seemed necessary to give page references.

1   W. L. Hildburgh, 'English Alabaster Carvings as Records of Medieval Religious Drama', *Archaeologia*, XCIII (1949), pp. 52–101; M. D. Anderson, *Drama and Imagery in English Medieval Churches* (Cambridge, 1963); Stella Mary Newton, *Renaissance Theatre Costume and the sense of the historic past* (London, 1975) and *Fashion in the Age of the Black Prince* (Boydell, 1980). Newton is a stage designer as well as a costume historian, and brings a practical eye to bear on her considerable scholarship: Hildburgh and Anderson are full of iconographic material but assume rather too readily that craftsmen copy 'real life' when all the evidence suggests that they copy other craftsmen: most of their theatrical illustrations are copies rather than parallels. Clifford Davidson, *Drama and Art* (see Abbreviations), a guide to a series of handbooks in progress, adopts the opposite view, that drama copies art, but perhaps rather too readily in its turn.

² See Meg Twycross and Sarah Carpenter 'Materials and Methods of Mask-making', *METh* 4:1 (1982), p. 39.

³ See Woolf, p. 117.

⁴ See J. K. Bonnell, 'The Serpent with a Human Head in Art and in Mystery Play', *American Journal of Archaeology*, XXI (1917), pp. 255–91.

⁵ R. W. Ingram, 'To find the players and all that longeth therto: Notes on the Production of Medieval Drama at Coventry', in *Elizabethan Theatre* v, ed. G. R. Hibbard (Macmillan 1975), pp. 17–44, and 'Pleyng geire accustumed belongyng & necessarie : guild records and pageant production at Coventry', in *Proceedings of the First Colloquium (REED*, Toronto, 1979), pp. 60–101. Peter Meredith's article "Item for a grone – iijd" – records and performance', pp. 26–60 in the same collection, is also very useful on this subject.

⁶ *York City Chamberlains' Account Rolls 1396–1500*, ed. R. B. Dobson (Surtees Society CVCII, Durham, 1980 for 1978 and 1979), pp. xxxii–xxxiv.

⁷ *REED Coventry*, p. 93 (Smiths, 1499), p. 25, p. 200, p. 474; 'Chelmsford', p. 108; *Malone VII*, p. 210; Chambers II, p. 396.

⁸ See the direction at line 343.

⁹ Ingram, 'Pleyng geire', p. 89.

¹⁰ 'Pleadings in a Theatrical Lawsuit: Rastell vs. Walton', in *XVth Century Prose and Verse*, ed. Edward Arber (London, 1903), pp. 307–321.

¹¹ Juan de Alcega, *Tailor's Pattern Book*, trans. Jean Pain and Cecilia Bainton (Bedford (Ruth Bean) 1979), fols. 36a–41a.

¹² See Philip Grierson, *English Linear Measures* (University of Reading Stenton Lecture 1971), p. 12; L. F. Salzman, *English Industries of the Middle Ages* (London, H. Pondes, 1964), pp. 198, 229–30.

¹³ Meg Twycross and Sarah Carpenter, 'Masks in Medieval English Theatre' *METh* 3:1 (1981), pp. 7–44; 3:2, pp. 69–113. I am preparing a lengthier note on the presentation of nakedness.

¹⁴ *Dives and Pauper*, Vol. 1 pt. 1, ed. Priscilla Heath Barnum, London (EETS OS 275), 1976, pp. 93–4.

¹⁵ Jacques Thiboust, *Relation de la Monstre du Mystère des SS. Actes des Apostres*, ed. Mᵉ. Labouvrie (Bourges, 1836), p. 25: *Saint Pierre, vestu d'une robe de satin cramoisy, broché d'or, enrichie de diamans et grosses perles, et manteau en écharpe de drap d'or frisé.*

¹⁶ I would like to thank Professor Alexandra Johnston for allowing me to use her transcriptions of the Eton College records made for her forthcoming *REED Berkshire* volume.

¹⁷ *Dives and Pauper*, vol. 1 pt. 1, pp. 94, 100–101.

The Shipwrights' Craft

Richard Beadle

¹ J. W. Robinson, '*Ad Majorem Dei Gloriam*', *Medieval Drama: A Collection of Festival Papers*, ed. W. Selz (Vermillion, 1968), pp. 31–7.

² Anna J. Mill, 'The Hull Noah Play', *Modern Language Review*, XXXIII (1938), pp. 489–505.

³ Woolf, pp. 132–145; Richard Axton, 'The Miracle Plays of Noah', *Medieval Literature: Chaucer and the Alliterative Tradition*, The New Pelican Guide to

English Literature, Vol. I, Pt. 1, ed. Boris Ford (Harmondsworth, 1982), pp. 277–89.

[4] For reproductions of early illustrations of Noah as a medieval shipwright see F. Moll, 'Der Schiffbaumeister in der Christlichen Kunst', *Gute Fahrt: Ein Wochenblatt für Schiffer*, XXVII: v (1930), pp. 5–7.

[5] Mill, 'The Hull Noah Play', pp. 497–503. Noah in the Newcastle Shipwrights' play uses the expression 'To clink yon nails twain' and God promises to furnish him with 'Pitch, tar, seam (*nail*), and rowe (*rove*)': *Non-Cycle Plays*, p. 26 line 26; p. 31 line 187. In the Chester 'Noyes Fludd', staged by the Waterleaders and Drawers of Dee, Noah alludes to various features of his vessel, such as mast, sail-yard, top-castle and bowsprit, and a well-known stage direction shows that his whole family mimed part of the work: 'Then Noe with all his familye shall make a signe as though the wrought upon the shippe with divers instruments'; see *Chester*, pp. 44–7, and p. 31 above.

[6] The following stage direction from the Noah episode in the sixteenth-century Cornish *Creacion of the World* shows that suitable properties could be provided: *Tooles and tymber redy, with planckys to make the Arcke: a beam, a mallet, a calkyn yre, ropes, mastes, pyche and tarr* (2254 sd.).

[7] There is a helpful account in J. P. Lewis, *A Study of the Interpretation of Noah and the Flood in Jewish and Christian Literature* (Leiden, 1968), pp. 158–167.

[8] O. Arngart, 'English *Craft* "a vessel" and some other Names for Vessels', *English Studies*, XXV (1943), pp. 161–9.

'Heven and Erthe in Lytyl Space'

Janet Cowen

[1] See David M. Robb, 'The Iconography of the Annunciation in the Fourteenth and Fifteenth Centuries', *Art Bulletin*, XVIII (1936), pp. 480–526; *Drama and Art*, p. 109.

[2] Cf. e.g. Woolf, p. 180; Kahrl, p. 54.

[3] See Henrik Cornell, *The Iconography of the Nativity of Christ*, (Uppsala, 1924).

[4] See *The Revelations of Saint Birgitta*, ed. W. P. Cumming (London (EETS), 1929), pp. xxix–xxxix.

[5] See J. W. Robinson, 'A Commentary on the York Play of the Birth of Jesus', *JEGP*, LXX (1971), pp. 241–54.

[6] Cf. Edward Hodnett, *English Woodcuts 1480–1535* (Oxford, 1973), nos. 625, 749, 777, 1428, 2095, 2139, 2284, 2363a. Examples have also been found in liturgical books of York Use produced abroad for use in England, see Clifford Davidson and David E. O'Connor, *York Art* (Kalamazoo, 1978), p. 48.

[7] For a survey of views see Tydeman, pp. 111–120.

[8] For the view that the stage directions are the author's own work see David Mills, op. cit. (p. 143, note 10).

[9] For the suggestion see Kahrl, p. 57.

[10] Ed. Frances A. Foster (London (EETS), 1926).

[11] Kahrl, p. 56.

[12] See Ruth Brant Davis, 'The Scheduling of the Chester Cycle Plays', *Theatre Notebook*, XXVII (1972/3), pp. 49–67; L. M. Clopper, 'The Rogers' Description of the Chester Plays', *Leeds Studies in English*, VII (1974), pp. 63–94;

L. M. Clopper, 'The Staging of the Medieval Plays of Chester: a Response', *Theatre Notebook*, XXVIII (1974), pp. 65–70; *REED Chester*, p. lvi.

[13] See D. S. Bland, 'The Chester "Nativity" One Play or Two?', *NQ*, CCVIII (1963), pp. 134–5; F. M. Salter, 'The banns of the Chester Plays', *RES*, XV (1939), pp. 432–57, and XVI (1940), pp. 1–17; pp. 137–48.

[14] For this analysis see 'N-Town', pp. xx–xxv. It has been supported by subsequent studies of the metre and style of the plays, and of the manuscript make-up and lay-out. See Stephen Spector, op. cit. (p. 143, note 6), and 'Symmetry in Watermark Sequences', *Studies in Bibliography, XXXI* (1978), pp. 162–78; *'N-Town' Facsimile*, p. vii.

[15] K. Cameron and Stanley J. Kahrl, 'Staging the N-Town Cycle', *Theatre Notebook, XXI* (1967), pp. 122–38 and pp. 152–65.

[16] Woolf, pp. 310–11.

[17] 'The Dramatic Setting of the Wakefield Annunciation', *PMLA*, LXXXI, no. 3(1966), pp. 193–8.

[18] For the complete text of this lyric see *A Selection of English Carols*, ed. R. L. Greene (Oxford, 1962), p. 107.

Producing Miracles
Darryll Grantley

[1] K. D. Uitti points out that 'in hagiographic literature the saint's renunciation of the world and his or her consequent dedication to divine love are often dramatically symbolized by a rejection of carnal love . . . The renunciation symbolizes the saint's acceptance and awareness of his status. It is therefore certainly no surprise to note that, in those saints' lives in which the saint's renunciation of earthly love is depicted with a particularly strong dramatic focus, the saint's miraculous powers consistently manifest themselves after he has denied his sexual instinct: the refusal of one kind of potency engenders another (*Story, Myth and Celebration in Old French Narrative Poetry* (Princeton, 1973), pp. 22–4).

[2] M. del Villar, 'Some Approaches to the Mediaeval English Saint's Play', *RORD*, XV–XVI (1972–3), p. 84.

[3] H. d'Outreman, *Histoire de la Ville et Comté de Valenciennes* (Douay, 1639), p. 396.

[4] Such a rear section screened by a curtain can be seen in Elie Konigson's conjectural plans of scaffolds for the Valenciennes Passion play of 1547 (based on contemporary drawings by Hubert Cailleau) in *La Répresentation d'un Mystère de la Passion à Valenciennes en 1547* (Paris, 1968), p. 42. Compare also Glynne Wickham's conjectural reconstruction of a pageant cart with its curtained off rear tiring-house (Wickham, p. 174).

[5] G. Cohen, ed. *Le Livre de Conduite du Régisseur et le Compte des Dépenses pour le Mystère de la Passion* (Paris, 1925), p. 96.

[6] See also Cailleau's miniature in G. Cohen, *Le Théatre en France au Moyen Age* (Paris, 1928), plate XLII (Procès de Paradis et Annonce à Marie).

[7] The Coventry Cappers and Drapers Companies, for examples, used windlasses in their pageants; see *REED Coventry*, pp. 220–1 and *passim*.

[8] Quoted in L. Petit de Julleville, *Les Mystères* (Paris, 1880), Vol. II, p. 103.

[9] B. Evans, *The Passion Play of Lucerne* (New York, 1943), p. 194, p. 211.

[10] Report by Philippe de Vigneulles of a Metz play of *La Sainte Hostie* quoted in Petit de Julleville, *Les Mystères*, p. 103.

[11] A. Jubinal, ed. *Mystères Inédits du Quinzième Siècle* (Paris, 1837), Vol. I, p. 27.

[12] G. Paris and G. Raynaud, ed., *Le Mystère de la Passion d'Arnoul Greban publiée d'après les manuscrits de Paris avec une Introduction et un Glossaire* (Paris, 1878), p. 172.

[13] Cohen, *Livre de Conduite*, p. 177.

The virtue of Perseverance

Richard Proudfoot

[1] *Percy's Reliques of ancient English Poetry*, Everyman's Library, Vol. I (London, 1906), p. 147.

[2] *Mirk's Festial*, ed. Theodor Erbe, (London (EETS ES 96), 1905), pp. 228–9.

[3] Peter Meredith, 'The Castle of Perseverance' in 'Census of Medieval Drama Productions', *RORD*, XXI (1978), p. 101.

[4] See S. C. Chew, *The Virtues Reconciled* (London, 1947).

[5] *Milton's Poems: Reproduced in Facsimile from the Manuscript in Trinity College, Cambridge* (Scholar Press, Merton, 1972), pp. 35, 40.

[6] Richard Southern, *The Medieval Theatre in the Round* (London, 1957).

[7] See, e.g., N. C. Schmitt, 'Was There a Medieval Theatre in the Round? A Re-examination of the Evidence', in J. Taylor and A. H. Nelson, ed., *Medieval English Drama* (Chicago, 1972).

[8] Meredith, 'The Castle of Perseverance', p. 100.

[9] David Mills, 'The Castle of Perseverance at Manchester', *METh* 3:1 (1981), pp. 55–6.

'Lusty fresch galaunts'

Tony Davenport

[1] On the representation of youth, worldliness, etc., in medieval literature see, M. W. Bloomfield, *The Seven Deadly Sins* (Michigan, 1952); B. Spivack, *Shakespeare and the Allegory of Evil* (New York & London, 1958); P. Tristram, *Figures of Life and Death in Medieval English Literature* (London, 1976).

[2] On costume see T. W. Craik, *The Tudor Interlude* (Leicester, 1958); G. Wickham, *Early English Stages 1300 to 1660: Vol. 3: Plays and their Makers to 1576* (London & Henley, 1981), Chap. V, section 4.

[3] On medieval satire see G. R. Owst, *Literature and Pulpit in Medieval England* (Cambridge, 1933); J. Peter, *Complaint and Satire in Early English Literature* (Oxford, 1956); V. J. Scattergood, *Politics and Poetry in the Fifteenth Century* (London, 1971).

[4] 'Huff! a galawnt!' is found in the late C15 MS Rawlinson 34.

[5] Peter Idley's *Instructions to his Son*, ed. C. d'Evelyn (Boston & London, 1935), Book IIB, lines 176ff. Caxton's *The Book of Curtesye*, ed. F. J. Furnivall, (London (EETS ES 3), 1868), lines 439ff.

6   'A Treatyse of a Galaunt' survives in three MSS. of late C15; one was printed in *Ballads from Manuscripts*, ed. F. J. Furnivall (London, 1868), Vol. I. It was printed three times during Henry VIII's reign by Wynkyn de Worde; this version is represented in *Early Popular Poetry of England*, ed. W. Carew Hazlitt (London, 1866), Vol. 3. The two versions are hereafter identified as A and B respectively. See *A Manual of the Writings in Middle English 1050–1500* (New Haven, Connecticut, 1975), Vol. 5, p. 1469.

7   See Rosemary Woolf, *The English Religious Lyric in the Middle Ages* (Oxford, 1968), p. 348.

8   Ian Lancashire, *Two Tudor Interludes* (Manchester, 1980), pp. 24–30.

9. Divine and human justice
Robert Potter

1   John Bellamy, *Crime and Public Order in England in the Later Middle Ages* (London, 1973), p. 188.

2   Alan Harding, *The Law Courts of Medieval England* (London, 1973), p. 47.

3   See John J. Molloy, *A Theological Interpretation of the Moral Play Wisdom, Who is Christ* (Washington D.C., 1952).

4   J. H. Baker, *An Introduction to English Legal History* (London, 1971), pp. 88–90.

5   Alexandra F. Johnston and Margaret Dorrell, 'The Doomsday Pageant of the York Mercers, 1433' and 'The York Mercers and their Pageant of Doomsday', *Leeds Studies in English*, NS V (1971), pp. 29–34 and VI (1973), pp. 10–35.

Editions of Plays Discussed

Where appropriate, cross-references are given to the list of Abbreviations on pp. vi–xii.

Calisto and Melibea	in J. S. Farmer, *Six Anonymous Plays*, series 1 (1905, republished Guildford, 1966).
Castle of Perseverance, The	see *Macro*, pp. 1–111.
Chester Plays	see *Chester*.
Conversion of St. Paul, The	see *Digby*, pp. 1–23.
Cornish Plays	see Norris (also *Creacion of the World, Meriasek*, below).
Coventry Plays	see *Coventry*.
Creacion of the World, The	*The Creacion of the World*, ed. Paula Neuss (Garland, 1983).
Croxton *Play of the Sacrament, The*	see *Non-cycle Plays*, pp. 58–89.
Everyman	*Everyman*, ed. A. C. Cawley (Manchester, 1961).
Fulgens and Lucrece	in *The Plays of Henry Medwall* ed. A. H. Nelson (Woodbridge, Suffolk, 1980).
Gentleness and Nobility	in J. S. Farmer, *The Writings of John Heywood* (1908, republished Guildford, 1966).
Hick Scorner	in *Two Tudor Interludes* ed. Ian Lancashire (Manchester University Press (Revels Plays), 1980).
Like Will to Like	in J. A. B. Somerset, *Four Tudor Interludes* (London, 1974).
Ludus Coventriae	see 'N-Town'.
Lusty Juventus	as for *Like Will to Like*.
Magnificence	John Skelton, *Magnificence*, ed. Paula Neuss (Manchester University Press (Revels Plays), 1980).
Mankind	see *Macro*, pp. 153–84.
Mary Magdalen	see *Digby*, pp. 24–95.
Meriasek	*Beunans Meriasek*, ed. Whitley Stokes, (London, 1872).

Mundus et Infans	in *Three Late Medieval Morality Plays* ed. G. A. Lester (London, 1981).
Nature	as for *Fulgens and Lucrece*.
Newcastle Shipwrights' Play	see *Non-cycle Plays*, pp. 19–31.
Norwich Grocers' Play	see *Non-cycle Plays*, pp. 8–18.
N-Town plays	see 'N-Town'.
Pride of Life, The	see *Non-cycle Plays*, pp. 90–105.
Respublica	ed. W. W. Greg (London (EETS OS 226), 1952).
Towneley plays	see *Towneley*.
Wakefield plays	see *Towneley*.
Wisdom	see *Macro*, pp. 113–52.
Youth	as for *Hick Scorner*.
York Plays	see *York*.

Quotations from Shakespeare's plays are taken from the New Arden editions.

Appendix

Glossary to lines 57–121 of York play VIII

64. *markis*	measurements (*MED*, mark(e n. (1), 4. (a) quotes this example of the term).
67. *shippe-crafte*	shipwrightry.
74. *be sware*	squarely.
of skwyn	obliquely, on a slant. (A rare word; this is the only instance of it quoted in the *OED*, *sb. squin*).
75. *burdes*	boards; the planks which go to make up the strakes running from stem to stern of a vessel (*ME Sea Terms* pp. 32–3).
wandes	long, thin pieces of wood; see *OED*, *wand*, sb., 3, for the use of 'wands' in constructions of various kinds. Their exact function in this context is not certain. As they go with the *burdes* they were evidently part of the hull, and may perhaps have been the 'laths or battens, particularly as used in covering the space, or seam, between two planks' mentioned in *ME Sea Terms*, p. 168.
77. *semes*	seams of the hull; 'interstice[s] between the planks in a vessel' (*ME Sea Terms*, p. 157); see also 105, *sewe*, below.
98. *lyne*	measuring-line (*MED*, line n. (1), 2 (b), quotes this example of the term.
100. *twyne*	probably = 'warp', 'twist'; *OED*, *twine*, v.¹, 6b, cites the word in this sense from 1601, in a carpentry context.
101. *june*	join (i.e. the *burde* (96) to another).
gynn	device, instrument; a specific tool may have been intended (*MED*, gin(ne n., 3. (a)).
102. *symonde*	cement; perhaps a substance used to seal the seams (*MED*, ciment n. (b)).
105. *sewe*	sew, the action of securing the *semes* between the *burdes*. 'In prehistoric shipbuilding in the North the planks were literally sewn together with sinews or withes, thus forming a seam' (*ME Sea Terms*, p. 158). By the York Noah's day iron nails were being used for this purpose: see next.
106. *cleyngked*	clenched, clinkered. This word describes the manner in which the *burdes* making up the hull were attached to one another and to the ribs of the vessel. *Revette*[s]

151

(109), rivets, nails, were driven through the *burdes* and their points turned over or flattened on *rewe*[s] (109), roves, which were small metal plates with holes, intended to prevent the rivets from springing out (*ME Sea Terms*, pp. 139, 151–2, 154–5).

110. *bowe*   This line is doubly difficult. The manuscript reads 'With þer bowe þer nowe wyrke I wele', and is evidently corrupt. The emendation printed above, 'þer þe bowe', suggests that *bowe* here means the bow or fore-end of the vessel, though the word in this sense is rare in English before the seventeenth century (*ME Sea Terms*, p. 37, however, quotes examples from as early as 1409). *Bowe* could also be a corruption of 'both', in which case an alternative emendation could lead to Noah's saying 'With both of these (? *sc.* the rivet and the rove) I now work skilfully'.

Index

General terms such as 'actor', 'audience', 'dialogue', 'staging' and 'stage-direction' will be found on almost every page of the book; similarly general references to 'mystery' and 'morality' plays are too copious to be indexed. Mystery plays are listed according to the titles in the editions we have used (see pp. 149–50); guilds responsible for the pageants have been given separate entries.

Magnificence, 114, 118, 122–3, 149
Somerset, J. A. B., 149
Southern, Richard, 105, 147
Southwark Cathedral, 106
Spector, Stephen, 143, 146
Spenser, Edmund, 96
Spivack, Bernard, 147
Stanzaic Life of Christ, A, 70
Stevens, John, 1, 3–4, 142
Stevens, Martin, xiv, 77
Suffolk, ix, xiii, 42, 143

tableaux vivants, 51
Taylor, Jerome, 147
Tewkesbury, 36
Tewkesbury Abbey, 106
Thiboust, Jacques, 144
Thomas of Chabham, 5
Three Ladies of London, 114
Thynne, Francis, 37
Titivillus, 93
Tormentors, 35, 37, 39, 41, 42, 46, 47
Toronto, ix
  University College of, 106
touring, 19, 103
Towneley plays, xiv, 150
  Annunciation, 63–4, 76, 77, 146
  Caesar Augustus, 64, 76
  Creation and Fall, 32, 77
  First Shepherds' Play, 77
  Judgement, 5, 21
  Nativity, 63–4
  Noah, 39, 50
  Offering of the Kings (Magi), 76
  Pharaoh, 64
  Pilgrims, 32
  Salutation of Elizabeth, 64, 77
  Second Shepherds' Play, 4, 93, 108, 130
  manuscripts of, xiv
'Treatise of a Galaunt', 115, 148
Trial of Treasure, The, 128
Trinity, the, 74, 136–7
Trinity College, Oxford, 106
Tristram, Phillipa, 147
Trowle, 3
Tyburn, 122, 125, 127
Tydeman, William, xiv, 5, 44, 91, 145
Twycross, Meg, x, 30, 62, 94, 143–4

Uitti, K. D., 146
Uriel, 82

Valenciennes Passion play, 80, 146
vexillatores, 20
Vice, the, 122, 134
Villar, M. del, 146

Vigneulles, Phillipe de, 147
Vyvyan, John, 42

waits, 4, 6, 35
  see also Hewet, James
Wakefield plays, *see* Towneley plays
Wall, Carolyn, 142
Westminster Hall, 133
Wickham, Glynne, xiv, 79, 85, 87, 90, 146, 147
Wisdom, 32, 80, 93–5, 103, 111, 112, 114, 119–21, 124, 127, 132–3, 148, 150
Woolf, Rosemary, xiv, 51, 144, 145, 148
Wright, Thomas, xv, 113, 119
Wygson, Mr, 41

York, Archbishop and Dean of, 16
York, city of, 30, 35, 40, 50, 144
York, Creed play, 40, 47, 92
York guilds:
  Bakers, 47
  Barkers, 42
  Bowyers and Fletchers, 23
  Cappers, 16
  Cardmakers and Fullers, 21–3
  Fishers and Mariners, 51
  Glovers, 16
  Ironmongers, 15
  Masons and Goldsmiths, 23, 41–2
  Mercers, 14, 22, 34–5, 39, 40, 42, 43, 139, 148
  Parchmenters and Bookbinders, 23
  Pewterers and Founders, 64
  Scriveners, 16–17, 143
  Shipwrights, 16, 50–61, 144–5
  Spicers, 64
  Tapiters and Couchers, 23
  Tilemakers, 23
  Tilethatchers, 64
  Vintners, 15
York Memorandum Book, 33–4
York Minster, 9
York plays, xv, 8, 43, 150
  Banns, 41, 48
    Ordo Paginarum, 15
    Annunciation and Visitation, 2, 63–5
    Ascension, 23
    Assumption of the Virgin, 6, 8–10
    Building of the Ark, 50–61, 144–5, 151–2
    Creation, 1, 42
    Crucifixion, 47
    Fall, 33
    Flood, 51
    Incredulity of Thomas, 16–17
    Joseph's Trouble about Mary, 63–6